FREE AND FAIR ELECTIONS: INTERNATIONAL LAW AND PRACTICE

FREE AND FAIR ELECTIONS: INTERNATIONAL LAW AND PRACTICE

Guy S. Goodwin-Gill

Inter-Parliamentary Union

Geneva

1994

ISBN 92 9142 000 X

Published by

INTER-PARLIAMENTARY UNION
B.P. 438
1211 Geneva 19
Switzerland

Printed and bound by Sadag Imprimerie, Bellegarde, France
Layout and typesetting by LB Publishing, Toronto, Canada
Cover design by Aloys Lolo, Les Studios Lolos, Carouge, Switzerland

Table of Contents

Foreword

The Universal Declaration of Human Rights, adopted in 1948 in the heady aftermath of the second world war, established that the election of representative institutions is the basis for the democratic management of public affairs. This general principle of the working of democracy has been subsequently reaffirmed in several texts of world-wide or regional scope. Until recently, however, States were deeply divided as to how it should be applied in practice.

Having now shed the qualifiers with which it was often weighted down in recent times, democracy has acquired a clearer and more precise meaning which has been generally accepted and whose acceptance will, it is to be hoped, both spread and mature.

Regular and genuine elections, through which the people have a real opportunity to choose their representatives freely, are now acknowledged to be the cornerstone of democracy. Hence, the increase in the number of elections of a pluralistic nature and the growing attention given by the world community to the conditions for the holding of those elections which, if they are really to satisfy the requirements of democracy, must be **free and fair**, in the accepted expression.

This international focus has taken the form of assistance in organizing elections and observing the electoral process. States, intergovernmental and non-governmental organizations and institutions of all kinds are taking part in this action on a hitherto unprecedented scale. The United Nations has set up a special unit for this purpose and the United Nations system as a whole is extremely active in this field.

It was only natural for the Inter-Parliamentary Union, which works for the firm establishment of representative institutions, to become actively involved. When defining its policy in this area, it placed the emphasis on normative action. Its governing bodies pointed in particular to a shortcoming which needed to be corrected: the absence of a clear and detailed definition of the constituent elements of a free and fair election. They therefore recommended that the Union undertake a study on this subject and suggested that the study could also serve as the basis for the drafting of a text expressing the consensus of the world-wide inter-parliamentary community on what is a free and fair electoral process.

The Union is now pleased to present the study which was entrusted to an independent consultant, Professor Guy S. Goodwin-Gill, of Carleton University (Canada). Entitled *Free and Fair Elections: International Law and Practice*, it seeks to establish the content of the rules and standards of international law, with special attention to State practice. It therefore makes selective and illustrative comparisons of electoral laws and practices and includes the experience of a number of observer and technical assistance missions to States in transition to representative democracy. The study covers the whole gamut of the electoral process from the electoral law to the balloting, monitoring of the poll, counting of ballots and proclamation of the results, including complaints and dispute resolution.

A first draft of the study prepared by Professor Goodwin-Gill was reviewed by the members of the Union's Consultative Committee of Experts at a meeting in Geneva in early December 1993. Based on their comments, the draft was revised and discussed at two separate meetings of experts, one in New York and the other in Paris. The experts, all of whom provided advice in their personal capacity, were in New York: Professor Reginald Austin, Director of the Legal and Constitutional Affairs Division in the Commonwealth Secretariat, Mr. Horacio Boneo, Director of the United Nations Electoral Assistance Unit, Mr. Larry Garber, Executive Assistant at the United States Agency for International Development, Dr. Ron Gould, Assistant Electoral Commissioner of Elections Canada, Dr. Jennifer McCoy, Professor at Georgia University and Senior Research Associate at the Carter Center, and Mr. Michael Stoddard of the National Democratic Institute for International Affairs; and in Paris: Mr. Michel Ameller, Honorary Secretary General of the French National Assembly, Professor Gérard Conac, Université de Paris I, Mrs. Christine Desouches from the Agency for Cultural and Technical Co-operation (ACCT), Mr. Jean-Philippe Fournet, from the French National Assembly Law Commission, Professor Jean Gicquel, Université de Paris I, Professor Jean-Claude Masclet, Dean of the Jean-Monnet Faculty at Université Paris-Sud, Dr. Didier Maus, Director of the International Institute for Public Administration (IIAP) and Mrs. Hélène Mazeran, responsible for studies on international relations at the IIAP.

The Inter-Parliamentary Union owes a debt of gratitude to all those who provided advice and assistance to the author during the preparation of this study. Special thanks are due to Mr. Boneo and Dr. Maus who were particularly helpful in organizing the two meetings in New York and Paris. The IPU is also grateful to the Ford Foundation for providing a grant covering some of the costs relating to this study. Last but not least, the Union is particularly indebted to Professor Goodwin-Gill for the quality of his study which remains entirely his work.

As foreseen, when the study was presented at the 91st Inter-Parliamentary Conference held in Paris in March 1994, the Union's governing bodies decided to use it as the basis for preparing a political declaration. A small drafting committee composed of members of parliament from all the geo-political regions was immediately established to finalize a text and, on the last day of the Conference, the Inter-Parliamentary Council unanimously adopted the *Declaration on Criteria for Free and Fair Elections.* The text of the Declaration, the first to express a world-wide political consensus on the subject, will be found immediately after this foreword.

Both the study and the Declaration make a substantial contribution to national and international thinking and action in the field of electoral processes. It is hoped that those who are responsible for organizing elections as well as those who come from countries near and far to observe them will find in these texts food for thought and guidance for their decisions.

Pierre Cornillon
Secretary General
Inter-Parliamentary Union
Geneva, April 1994

DECLARATION ON CRITERIA FOR FREE AND FAIR ELECTIONS

Unanimously adopted by the Inter-Parliamentary Council at its 154th session (Paris, 26 March 1994)*

THE INTER-PARLIAMENTARY COUNCIL,

Reaffirming the significance of the Universal Declaration of Human Rights and the International Covenant on Civil and Political Rights which establish that the authority to govern shall be based on the will of the people as expressed in periodic and genuine elections,

Acknowledging and endorsing the fundamental principles relating to periodic free and fair elections that have been recognized by States in universal and regional human rights instruments, including the right of everyone to take part in the government of his or her country directly or indirectly through freely chosen representatives, to vote in such elections by secret ballot, to have an equal opportunity to become a candidate for election, and to put forward his or her political views, individually or in association with others,

Conscious of the fact that each State has the sovereign right, in accordance with the will of its people, freely to choose and develop its own political, social, economic and cultural systems without interference by other States in strict conformity with the United Nations Charter,

Wishing to promote the establishment of democratic, pluralist systems of representative government throughout the world,

Recognizing that the establishment and strengthening of democratic processes and institutions is the common responsibility of governments, the electorate and organized political forces, that periodic and genuine elections are a necessary and indispensable element of sustained efforts to protect the rights and interests of the governed and that, as a matter of practical experience, the right of everyone to take part in the government of his or her country is a crucial factor in the effective enjoyment by all of human rights and fundamental freedoms,

Welcoming the expanding role of the United Nations, the Inter-Parliamentary Union, regional organizations and parliamentary assemblies, and international and national non-governmental organizations in providing electoral assistance at the request of governments,

Therefore adopts the following Declaration on Free and fair Elections, and *urges* Governments and Parliaments throughout the world to be guided by the principles and standards set out therein:

---

*   Of the Union's 129 Member Parliaments, 112 were represented at the Conference when this Declaration was adopted.

1. **Free and Fair Elections**
   In any State the authority of the government can only derive from the will of the people as expressed in genuine, free and fair elections held at regular intervals on the basis of universal, equal and secret suffrage.

2. **Voting and Elections Rights**
   (1) Every adult citizen has the right to vote in elections, on a non-discriminatory basis.

   (2) Every adult citizen has the right to access to an effective, impartial and non-discriminatory procedure for the registration of voters.

   (3) No eligible citizen shall be denied the right to vote or disqualified from registration as a voter, otherwise than in accordance with objectively verifiable criteria prescribed by law, and provided that such measures are consistent with the State's obligations under international law.

   (4) Every individual who is denied the right to vote or to be registered as a voter shall be entitled to appeal to a jurisdiction competent to review such decisions and to correct errors promptly and effectively.

   (5) Every voter has the right to equal and effective access to a polling station in order to exercise his or her right to vote.

   (6) Every voter is entitled to exercise his or her right equally with others and to have his or her vote accorded equivalent weight to that of others.

   (7) The right to vote in secret is absolute and shall not be restricted in any manner whatsoever.

3. **Candidature, Party and Campaign Rights and Responsibilities**
   (1) Everyone has the right to take part in the government of their country and shall have an equal opportunity to become a candidate for election. The criteria for participation in government shall be determined in accordance with national constitutions and laws and shall not be inconsistent with the State's international obligations.

   (2) Everyone has the right to join, or together with others to establish, a political party or organization for the purpose of competing in an election.

   (3) Everyone individually and together with others has the right:
   - To express political opinions without interference;
   - To seek, receive and impart information and to make an informed choice;
   - To move freely within the country in order to campaign for election;
   - To campaign on an equal basis with other political parties, including the party forming the existing government.

   (4) Every candidate for election and every political party shall have an equal opportunity of access to the media, particularly the mass communications media, in order to put forward their political views.

(5) The right of candidates to security with respect to their lives and property shall be recognized and protected.

(6) Every individual and every political party has the right to the protection of the law and to a remedy for violation of political and electoral rights.

(7) The above rights may only be subject to such restrictions of an exceptional nature which are in accordance with law and reasonably necessary in a democratic society in the interests of national security or public order (*ordre public*), the protection of public health or morals or the protection of the rights and freedoms of others and provided they are consistent with States' obligations under international law. Permissible restrictions on candidature, the creation and activity of political parties and campaign rights shall not be applied so as to violate the principle of non-discrimination on grounds of race, colour, sex, language, religion, political or other opinion, national or social origin, property, birth or other status.

(8) Every individual or political party whose candidature, party or campaign rights are denied or restricted shall be entitled to appeal to a jurisdiction competent to review such decisions and to correct errors promptly and effectively.

(9) Candidature, party and campaign rights carry responsibilities to the community. In particular, no candidate or political party shall engage in violence.

(10) Every candidate and political party competing in an election shall respect the rights and freedoms of others.

(11) Every candidate and political party competing in an election shall accept the outcome of a free and fair election.

4. The Rights and Responsibilities of States

(1) States should take the necessary legislative steps and other measures, in accordance with their constitutional processes, to guarantee the rights and institutional framework for periodic and genuine, free and fair elections, in accordance with their obligations under international law. In particular, States should :

- Establish an effective, impartial and non-discriminatory procedure for the registration of voters;
- Establish clear criteria for the registration of voters, such as age, citizenship and residence, and ensure that such provisions are applied without distinction of any kind;
- Provide for the formation and free functioning of political parties, possibly regulate the funding of political parties and electoral campaigns, ensure the separation of party and State, and establish the conditions for competition in legislative elections on an

equitable basis;
- Initiate or facilitate national programmes of civic education, to ensure that the population are familiar with election procedures and issues.

(2) In addition, States should take the necessary policy and institutional steps to ensure the progressive achievement and consolidation of democratic goals, including through the establishment of a neutral, impartial or balanced mechanism for the management of elections. In so doing, they should, among other matters:
- Ensure that those responsible for the various aspects of the election are trained and act impartially, and that coherent voting procedures are established and made known to the voting public;
- Ensure the registration of voters, updating of electoral rolls and balloting procedures, with the assistance of national and international observers as appropriate;
- Encourage parties, candidates and the media to accept and adopt a Code of Conduct to govern the election campaign and the polling period;
- Ensure the integrity of the ballot through appropriate measures to prevent multiple voting or voting by those not entitled thereto;
- Ensure the integrity of the process for counting votes.

(3) States shall respect and ensure the human rights of all individuals within their territory and subject to their jurisdiction. In time of elections, the State and its organs should therefore ensure :
- That freedom of movement, assembly, association and expression are respected, particularly in the context of political rallies and meetings;
- That parties and candidates are free to communicate their views to the electorate, and that they enjoy equality of access to State and public-service media;
- That the necessary steps are taken to guarantee non-partisan coverage in State and public-service media.

(4) In order that elections shall be fair, States should take the necessary measures to ensure that parties and candidates enjoy reasonable opportunities to present their electoral platform.

(5) States should take all necessary and appropriate measures to ensure that the principle of the secret ballot is respected, and that voters are able to cast their ballots freely, without fear or intimidation.

(6) Furthermore, State authorities should ensure that the ballot is conducted so as to avoid fraud or other illegality, that the security and the integrity of the process is maintained, and that ballot counting is

undertaken by trained personnel, subject to monitoring and/or impartial verification.

(7) States should take all necessary and appropriate measures to ensure the transparency of the entire electoral process including, for example, through the presence of party agents and duly accredited observers.

(8) States should take the necessary measures to ensure that parties, candidates and supporters enjoy equal security, and that State authorities take the necessary steps to prevent electoral violence.

(9) States should ensure that violations of human rights and complaints relating to the electoral process are determined promptly within the timeframe of the electoral process and effectively by an independent and impartial authority, such as an electoral commission or the courts.

Author's Preface

Behind the face of the authority that represents the State lies one of the most troubling paradoxes in the modern system of international law and organization. The internal and external aspects of government are in tension: The State claims membership and the benefits of a relatively ordered society, yet insists that the basic principles of internal organization are not appropriate for international regulation. Though this may seem inevitable within a community of nations premised on sovereignty and equality, the modern history of international law provides ample evidence of its increasing insistence on the *internal* dimension to State responsibility. This Study attempts to present one element in that changing picture, focusing on the criteria for free and fair elections, considered from an international law perspective.

Researching and writing this work has been especially satisfying at the personal level. It provided an opportunity to learn from and take advantage of the extensive experience and critical judgment of the many individuals, mentioned above in the Foreword of the Secretary General, who participated in the expert meetings that examined earlier drafts. It also allowed me to appreciate at first hand the work now being undertaken by the Inter-Parliamentary Union and Parliamentarians around the world in the elections field, and generally in strengthening representative institutions.

I have especially appreciated the encouragement, co-operation and support extended to me by the IPU and its staff throughout the period of my work. I am very grateful, in particular, to Pierre Cornillon, Secretary General of the IPU, for his vision, his vast experience and his drive. The deep commitment he brings to the subject is an inspiration, as is his unflagging good humour. I owe a special debt as well to Anders B. Johnsson, Deputy Secretary General of the IPU. Equally enthusiastic, he facilitated contacts with those whose knowledge was fundamental to this review of State practice; he followed progress keenly and closely, readily shared his own experiences with election monitoring and observation missions, and was always on hand with suggestions and helpful advice. It has been a pleasure to work with them both.

Although many have made important and substantive contributions to this Study for the Inter-Parliamentary Union, the conclusions drawn and the opinions expressed are my own, and I alone am responsible for any errors and omissions.

Guy S. Goodwin-Gill
Geneva
April 1994

1.   INTRODUCTION AND OBJECTIVES

The ideal of democracy and the right of everyone to participate in the government of his or her country are clearly set out in article 21 of the 1948 Universal Declaration of Human Rights. Specifically, the provision in article 21(3) that 'the will of the people shall be the basis of the authority of government' stands as a straightforward statement of the principle of representative democracy, which is now increasingly seen as essential to the *legitimation* of governments among the community of States. Existing universal and regional human rights instruments, however, provide little detailed guidance on key issues, such as the periodicity of elections, the organization and entitlements of political parties, voter rights and registration, or the conduct of the ballot. That elections should allow expression of the 'will of the people' may offer a standard of effectiveness, but the ways and means by which progress towards that standard can be measured remain variable.

Political rights, such as the freedom to hold opinions, and to meet and exchange ideas and information, are central to the consolidation of democratic government and the rule of law. International institutions, however, such as the UN Commission on Human Rights and regional supervisory organizations, have done relatively little to develop either the conceptual foundations of these rights, or the practical application of the rights of participation. At the same time, the active involvement of the United Nations, the Inter-Parliamentary Union and a variety of inter-governmental and non-governmental organizations in election monitoring and technical assistance at the field level, is even now producing a body of practice that is contributing to the consolidation of norms and practices.

Still, there is a pressing need for clear criteria by which to judge whether elections are free and fair. In part, this will serve the interests of election monitors by enabling them to move beyond overly simplified gestures of approval or condemnation; but more importantly, such criteria are likely to increase national and international confidence in the electoral process, by reducing the necessity for challenge, limiting the possibilities for the arbitrary rejection of election results, and facilitating the transfer of power.

Terms like 'periodic', 'free', 'fair', and 'genuine', have no easily verifiable content, often being used subjectively, in an appeal to those assumed to share basic values and outlooks. In practice, it may be easier to identify what is not a free, fair or genuine election, by focusing on evidence of overt external influence, the lack of meaningful choice in single candidate and single party systems, or terrorisation of the electorate.

The objective of this study, however, is to get beyond presumptive or subjective assessments, to present a catalogue that is inductive, rather than deductive, and as capable of objective application as possible. The aim is thus to show what international law requires, drawing on existing rules and standards, but with special concentration also on the practice of States, including a selective and illustrative comparison of recent electoral laws and practices. In addition, the experiences of a number of observer and technical assistance missions to States in transition to representative democracy are considered, including the 'new' activities which the United Nations is now pursuing through the Electoral Assistance Unit established in 1992. The impact of these potentially norm-creating activities is also examined in the light of State sovereignty claims and concerns, bearing in mind article 2(7) of the UN Charter.[1] The ultimate question is whether any consensus exists on common standards, and how relevant are the variations or deviations, considered from an international law perspective.

One advantage of an international approach that draws upon comparative experience lies in its capacity to integrate variations in historical and cultural circumstance, and to accommodate different ways of determining what it is that the people choose. At the same time, international law's scheme of basic rules provides a number of organizing principles around which to assess, for example, the 'validity' of national legislation and practice, considered in terms of their contribution to the effective implementation of international obligations.

What is often forgotten is how recent are many of the electoral rights now taken for granted. 'Universal suffrage', which is rarely universal in practice, is a creature of the twentieth century. Only with the 1918 Representation of the People Act in the United Kingdom, for example, did most men over twenty-one obtain the vote, together then with women over thirty, who were not treated equally with male electors in regard to age until 1928; in Switzerland, many women went on waiting for the vote until 1991. Another recent candidate for universal application is the secret ballot; in 1948, the Universal Declaration of Human Rights also contemplated

1   See below, sections 2.2 and 2.4.

'equivalent free voting procedures', a phrase not found in article 25 of the 1966 Covenant on Civil and Political Rights.[2] Similarly, the current emphasis on voter registration and the prohibition of 'gerrymandering'[3] were accepted only belatedly in some of the so-called established democracies, including Northern Ireland and the southern United States.

Changes happen fast, however. In 1989, for the first time a revolutionary government that had come to power after a protracted armed struggle 'voluntarily' ceded power to the victor in an internationally monitored election.[4] In other regions, the process of democratization is gathering momentum, although in many cases it may be some time before the people find faith in the new institutions.

1.1 Outline of the Study

This study aims to present the international law dimensions to the *criteria* and *conditions* for the conduct of free and fair elections, showing what States have assumed in the way of obligation, and what may be required to ensure that such obligations are effectively implemented. The primary focus is on elections for legislative bodies, and only incidentally on presidential elections and referenda. Also, the study does not deal in detail with the choice of *electoral system*, that is, with the relative merits of majoritarian and proportional representation schemes. Although that choice bears directly on the 'value' of the vote and on the character of the legislature, it has for long been considered to fall exclusively within the realm of domestic jurisdiction. In other cases, the study does try to identify the acceptable range of variation in this area which is so clearly dominated by historical, cultural, political and social factors, and so close to the essential idea of the State as sovereign entity.

The study is divided into four principal sections. Following the present Introduction, Section 2 examines the international law background to the concept of free and fair elections, the relevance of the principle of self-determination, and the treatment accorded the subject by universal and regional human rights treaties. Bearing in mind the importance of *practice* in standard-setting, what States and others actually say and do, the section

2   But see section 7 of the CSCE Copenhagen Document; below, section 2.6.
3   The word comes from Governor Elbridge Gerry, for his division of an electoral district in Massachusetts in 1812 for party purposes.
4   See Council of Freely Elected Heads of Government, *Observing Nicaragua's Elections, 1989-1990.* Special Report #1, (1990), 34.

winds up with a brief review of recent UN, IPU and regional activity.

Section 3, which constitutes the bulk of the study, examines the 'constituent elements' in a system of free and fair elections: law and administration, including constituency delimitation and electoral commissions; voter rights and voter registration; civic education and voter information; candidates, political parties and political organization; electoral campaigns, including human rights and the election environment, media access and coverage; balloting, monitoring and results; and briefly, complaints and dispute resolution. The section finishes with a summary evaluation of recent experience in the field of election observation, showing wherever possible the commonality of principles and standards between established and emergent democracies.

Finally, Section 4 attempts to bring together the essential elements which international law proposes as the basis for a system of representative government, founded on periodic, free and fair elections. At the same time, due regard is paid to the self-evident truth that there is no single electoral model suitable for every country, but that each must forge the system most appropriate to realising the will of the people in a particular social, historical and cultural context. This section is roughly divided between principles and process, identifying, on the one hand, the area of absolute or qualified obligations; and, on the other hand, the mechanisms of implementation, the details of which may vary between States, but whose objectives are essentially the same.

1.2 Sources

A number of quite different 'sources' have been used in the course of this study and call for explanation, if only to signal awareness of the distinction between what the law is and what the law ought to be.

First, the study draws in particular upon relevant *international texts*, the most important of which are reproduced in Annex 1. They include treaties, which establish international obligations between the parties; formal declarations by States in international and regional bodies; and resolutions, such as those adopted by the UN General Assembly. Secondly, selected practice is used, the material sources for which include State legislation, the practice of international organizations, executive and judicial decisions. Thirdly, as 'secondary' evidence, the reports of United Nations, Commonwealth and other international observer missions sent to 'verify' or monitor the conduct of elections have been relied on, focusing on situations of transition from one-party authoritarian rule to a multi-party system, or on the implementation of the election component in internationally-brokered peace arrangements. Although international observer missions are increasingly a subject for standard-setting,[5] the value of such reports clearly varies. Where appropriate, the terms of reference of such mission are described, together with their findings on local law and practice. At their best, which often means where corroborated, election observer reports give clear information on law and administrative practice, indicating also the extent to which the *State* does or does not conduct itself in the elections context in accordance with international rules and standards, and whether the national process as a whole approaches the ideal of a free and fair election. It must be emphasized that international law gives no right to observe an election, and does not require any State to submit its electoral process to a system of international 'validation'; neither is it the case, however, that national elections are still exclusively a matter for the reserved domain of domestic jurisdiction.[6]

---

5   See, for example, Norwegian Helsinki Committee. Norwegian Institute of Human Rights. *Manual for Election Observation*. Mimeo. Draft. Oslo, (1993); and below.
6   See Gros Espiell, H., 'Liberté des Elections et Observation Internationale des Elections,' Mimeo., Conférence international de la Laguna, Tenerife, 27 févr.-2 mars 1994. Following a review of the Inter-American System in particular, he concludes: 'Dans le droit international d'aujourd'hui tant sur le plan universel que, selon le cas à l'échelle régionale, européenne et américaine, l'organisation d'élections libres, authentiques, pluralistes et périodiques, constitue une obligation internationalement exigible. Cette question est sortie du cadre exclusif de la juridiction interne et du domaine réservé aux Etats.'

2. THE INTERNATIONAL LAW BACKGROUND

Before reviewing in more detail the provisions of international and regional human rights instruments relating to elections, two preliminary issues call for comment: First, the nature of the international obligations involved; and secondly, the relationship of international election norms to the principles of self-determination and sovereignty.

2.1 International Obligations

The individual's right to take part in government, either directly of through freely chosen representatives, and the principle that the will of the people shall be expressed in periodic and genuine elections, reflect what are called 'obligations of result'.[1] States undertake to achieve a specific result, but enjoy substantial choice of means in determining which path they will follow to reach the internationally required objective. Whether a State has fulfilled an obligation of result depends on the means chosen for implementation, but also on what actually happens in practice; hence the critical importance of election monitoring. The standard of achievement remains an international one, however, while the choice of means in the electoral field is significantly *structured* by the specific reference in the key human rights instruments to underlying principles of non-discrimination, universal and equal suffrage and secret ballot.

2.2 Self-determination and National Sovereignty

The modern concept of self-determination established itself firmly in the anti-colonialist practice of the United Nations. The UN Charter, for example, declares the basic objectives of the trusteeship system to include promoting the progressive development of the inhabitants of the trust territories 'towards self-government or independence as may be appropriate to the particular circumstances of each territory and its peoples *and the freely expressed wishes of the people concerned.*'[2] Today, a number of commentators see the principle of self-determination as having both an external and an internal aspect. Cassese has thus described 'internal' or 'political self-determination' as meaning, among other matters, that a

---

1 For further discussion see, Goodwin-Gill, G.S., 'Obligations of Conduct and Result,' in P. Alston and K. Tomasevski, eds., *The Right to Food*, (1985), 111-8.
2 Art. 76(b), UN Charter.

people in a sovereign State can elect and keep the government of its choice.[3] He notes that the San Francisco Conference on International Organization in 1945 spoke of self-determination as reflecting the 'free and genuine expression of the will of the people',[4] but that the political context of such views was not broad enough at the time to include a claim to representative or democratic government

In later years, self-determination played a major part in the ball-game between 'socialist' and 'western' approaches to international relations, with emphasis in the UN falling then on colonialism and racist regimes. In due course, article 1 common to the 1966 Covenants on Civil and Political Rights and on Economic, Social and Cultural Rights, appeared to acknowledge a broader field of application for the principle:

> All peoples have the right of self-determination. By virtue of that right they freely determine their political status and freely pursue their economic, social and cultural development.

The scope and terminology remain ambiguous, however. Did this provision apply only to the rapidly diminishing number of peoples under colonial rule? Or was it a statement of the entitlement of all peoples to determine their 'collective political status' through democratic means?[5]

The 1970 Declaration on Principles of International Law concerning Friendly Relations and Co-operation among States added a further wrinkle to the fabric, with its implicit conditioning of self-determination on possession of 'a government representing the whole people...without distinction as to race, creed or colour.'[6] Other references to the right of all peoples 'freely to determine, without external interference,' their political status could nevertheless be interpreted restrictively, and as saying nothing about the conditions in which that will might be expressed. Although having a particular regional focus, the Final Act of the 1975 Helsinki Conference on Security and Co-operation in Europe offered a more encompassing approach, with its implicit linkage of self-determination to democratic

---

3 Cassese, A., 'Political Self-Determination—Old Concepts and New Developments,' in Cassese, A., ed., *UN Law/Fundamental Rights*, (1979), 137-65.

4 See sources cited ibid., 138-9.

5 Franck, T.M., 'The Emerging Right to Democratic Governance,' 86 *AJIL* 46, 58-9 (1992) (hereafter, Franck, 'Democratic Governance').

6 UNGA res. 2625(XXV), 24 Oct. 1970, Annex, Principle (e); Cassese, above note 3, at 143.

choice:[7]

>...all peoples always have the right, *in full freedom*, to determine, when
>and as they wish, their internal and external political status, without
>external interference...

Cassese again considers it clear from the *travaux préparatoires* that this phrase represents the triumph of 'the "Western" view, whereby the right of self-determination cannot be implemented if basic human rights and fundamental freedoms are not ensured to all members of the people concerned.' Thus, there can be no 'real choice' under an authoritarian government, or in the absence of freedom from internal interference such as oppression. What the Helsinki Conference brought to the fore was the 'anti-authoritarian, democratic thrust of self-determination.'[8]

Leaving aside the problematic disregard of the claims of minorities, the general argument can be supported by reference to Article 7 of the 'Algiers Declaration on the Rights of Peoples,' adopted in 1976 by an *ad hoc* non-governmental conference, which proclaims the 'right to have a democratic government representing all the citizens without distinction as to race, sex, belief or colour'.[9] To the representative non-racist government would now be added a non-discriminatory, democratic and human rights-protecting dimension.[10] In Cassese's words,[11]

>internal political self-determination does not mean generic
>self-government, but rather (a) the right to choose freely a government,

7   Helsinki Conference on Security and Co-operation in Europe, 1975, Principle VIII; text in 1975 *Digest of United States Practice in International Law*, pp. 8, 10.

8   Cassese, above note 3, 152-3.

9   Text in Cassese, A. and Jouve, E., eds., *Pour un droit des peuples: Essais sur la Déclaration d'Alger*, (1978), 27-30. Art. 7: 'Tout peuple a droit à un régime démocratique répresentant l'ensemble des citoyens, sans distinction de race, de sexe, de croyance ou de couleur et *capable d'assurer le respect effectif des droits de l'homme* et des libertés fondamentales pour tous.' (emphasis supplied).

10   Cf. Gaja, G., 'L'autodetermination politique dans la Déclaration d'Alger: objectifs et réalités,' in Cassese, A. & Jouve, E.., eds, *Pour un droit des peuples*, (1978), 124: 'Dans la mesure où un droit est véritablement attribué au peuple...l'existence d'un régime democratique doit également être considérée comme necessaire pour que le gouvernement puisse exercer le droit appartenant au peuple. En d'autre termes, le peuple n'est répresenté par le gouvernement que si le régime a un caractère démocratique.'

11   Cassese, 'Self-Determination,' above note 3, 154. See also Cassese, A., 'The Self-Determination of Peoples,' in Henkin, L., ed., *The International Bill of Rights-The International Covenant on Civil and Political Rights*, (1981), 92-113, at 97; Steiner, H.J., 'Political Participation as a Human Right,' 1 *Harv. HRY* 77-134 (1988).

exercising all the freedoms which make the choice possible (freedom of speech, or association, etc.) and (b) the right that the government, once chosen, continues to enjoy the consensus of the people and is neither oppressive nor authoritarian.

Other commentators are more sanguine, particularly where the 'rights of peoples' appear to be set against the rights of States at a certain normative level. Brownlie, for example, recognizes a 'core of reasonable certainty' in the principle: 'the right of a community which has a distinct character to have this character reflected in the institutions of government under which it lives'.[12] He doubts, however, that States have accepted rules going beyond this point, particularly when practice and the level of obligation at inter-State level are reviewed.[13] While accepting that self-determination is a right of 'peoples', rather than governments, Crawford nevertheless considers it 'axiomatic that international law does not guarantee representative, still less democratic governments'.[14] On the other hand, '[t]o the extent that it applies, it qualifies the right of governments to dispose of the "peoples" in question in ways which conflict with their rights to self-determination.'[15]

The precise relationship of self-determination and 'election rights' will remain controversial, so long as the connection is seen as likely to 'internationalize' political opposition. Not surprisingly, a number of States use self-determination in self-defence against increasing international and United Nations activity in the election field. For example, allegations of irregularities in the 1986 Mexican elections were brought before the Inter-American Commission on Human Rights, claiming violation, among others, of the free exercise of political rights set forth in the 1969 Pact of San José. The Government of Mexico argued that the Commission had no jurisdiction to give a decision on electoral processes, for reasons of national sovereignty and the right of self-determination.[16] The Commission

12   Brownlie, I., 'The Rights of Peoples in Modern International Law,' in Crawford, J., ed., *The Rights of Peoples*, (1988), 1, at 5.
13   Ibid., at 12.
14   Crawford, J., 'The Rights of Peoples: "Peoples" or "Governments"?' in Crawford, J., ed., *The Rights of Peoples*, (1988), 55.
15   Ibid., at 59.
16   Final Report on Cases 9768, 9780 et 9828 : IACmHR 97, OEA/Ser. L/V/II, doc. 7, rév. 1 (1990); Buergenthal, T. and Norris, R.E., eds, *Human Rights : The Inter-American System*, Pt. 3, Cases and Decisions, (1993), 97.

disagreed, holding that by having signed and ratified the Convention, Mexico had consented to certain aspects of its internal jurisdiction being subject to judgment by organs set up to protect the rights recognized:

> The IACHR is also empowered to verify, with respect to those rights, if the holding of periodic, authentic elections, with universal, equal, and secret suffrage takes place, within the framework of the necessary guarantees so that the results represent the popular will, including the possibility that the voters could, if necessary, effectively appeal against an electoral process that they consider fraudulent, defective and irregular or that ignores the 'right to access, under general conditions of equality, to the public functions of the country.'

The objection of sovereignty nevertheless continues to be raised. United Nations General Assembly resolution 46/130, for example, on 'Respect for the principles of national sovereignty and non-interference in the internal affairs of States in their electoral processes,' seeks to reaffirm that,[17]

> it is the concern solely of peoples to determine methods and to establish institutions regarding the electoral process, as well as to determine the ways for its implementation according to their constitution and national legislation.

The same words were adopted in the equivalent resolutions for 1992 and 1993, save that the most recent version added the significant qualifier, 'that, consequently, States should establish the necessary mechanisms and means to guarantee full popular participation in these processes.'[18]

The international 'election rights' that are the subject of this paper are not new, however.[19] They represent the developed content of rights already established, although it cannot be excluded that this process of

---

17   UNGA res. 46/130, 17 Dec. 1991, adopted by 102 votes in favour, 40 against, with 13 abstentions. See further below, section 2.4.

18   See UNGA res. 48/124, 20 Dec. 1993, para. 2, adopted by 101 votes in favour, 51 against and 17 abstentions; cf. UNGA res. 47/130, 18 Dec. 1992, adopted by 99 votes in favour, 45 against, with 16 abstentions.

19   Consequently they should not fall foul of Brownlie's strictures ('a part of the proliferation of academic inventions of new human rights and the launching of new normative candidates by anyone who can find an audience': 'The Rights of Peoples,' above note 12, at 12). Also Alston, P., 'Conjuring up New Human Rights: A Proposal for Quality Control,' 78 *AJIL* 607 (1984).

consolidation will have novel consequences in other areas of international law and organization, such as sovereignty, legitimacy, membership and international representation. In its internal aspect, self-determination can be read as stating the same objective as is reflected in the principle of free and fair or genuine elections that the will of the people shall be the basis of the authority of government. In view of its ambiguous provenance, however, the principle of self-determination may best be left aside for the present, at least so far as it may permit a deductive argument for electoral rights. Rather, attention should be paid to those specific obligations in the matter of elections already assumed by States, and to the equally accepted political human rights that may reasonably be linked thereto. In the final analysis, to say that a nation enjoys or does not enjoy the right of self-determination may be no more than a validating or invalidating judgment on a complex process.

2.3 Elections and Human Rights Treaties

2.3.1 Universal instruments

Article 21 of the 1948 Universal Declaration of Human Rights, summarised above, sets out the basic premises for 'election rights,' which were later developed in article 25 of the 1966 Covenant on Civil and Political Rights:

> Every citizen shall have the right and the opportunity, without any of the distinctions mentioned in article 2 and without unreasonable restrictions:
> (a) To take part in the conduct of public affairs, directly or through freely chosen representatives;
> (b) To vote and to be elected at genuine periodic elections which shall be by universal and equal suffrage and shall be held by secret ballot, guaranteeing the free expression of the will of the electors;
> (c) To have access, on general terms of equality, to public service in his country.

Such a formal provision might be of little substantive impact, however, were it not for the 'political and campaign rights' that are 'critical to a meaningful election process.'[20] Articles 19, 21 and 22 are particularly relevant:

20   Larry Garber and Clark Gibson, *Review of United Nations Electoral Assistance 1992-93*, (Aug. 1993) (hereafter Garber & Gibson, *Electoral Assistance*), 58; cf. Franck, 'Democratic Governance,' at 61: 'the essential preconditions for an open electoral process'.

Article 19

1. Everyone shall have the right to hold opinions without interference.

2. Everyone shall have the right to freedom of expression; this right shall include freedom to seek, receive and impart information and ideas of all kinds, regardless of frontiers, either orally, in writing or in print, in the form of art, or through any other media of his choice.

3. The exercise of the rights provided for in paragraph 2 of this article carries with it special duties and responsibilities. It may therefore be subject to certain restrictions, but these shall only be such as are provided by law and are necessary:

(a) For respect of the rights or reputations of others;

(b) For the protection of national security or of public order (*ordre public*), or of public health or morals.

Article 21

The right of peaceful assembly shall be recognized. No restrictions may be placed on the exercise of this right other than those imposed in conformity with the law and which are necessary in a democratic society in the interests of national security or public safety, public order (*ordre public*), the protection of public health or morals or the protection of the rights and freedoms of others.

Article 22

1. Everyone shall have the right to freedom of association with others, including the right to form and join trade unions for the protection of his interests.

2. No restrictions may be placed on the exercise of this right other than those which are prescribed by law and which are necessary in a democratic society in the interests of national security or public safety, public order (*ordre public*), the protection of public health or morals or the protection of the rights and freedoms of others...

These political rights, coupled with the collective entitlement to free and fair elections, together offer a legal basis for a claim to representative government.

2.3.2 Regional instruments

The idea of popular government is common also to the African Charter on Human and Peoples' Rights,[21] the American Convention on Human Rights,[22] and the European Convention on Human Rights. The Preamble to the latter Convention reaffirms the 'profound belief' of the contracting States, 'in those Fundamental Freedoms which are the foundations of justice and peace in the world and are best maintained...by an effective political democracy.' Electoral rights did not figure in the body of the Convention, however, given substantial disagreement between the Consultative Assembly and the Committee of Ministers.[23] A much watered-down provision eventually appeared in the First Protocol, article 3 of which declares what was clearly intended to be a limited inter-State obligation:

> The High Contracting Parties undertake to hold free elections at reasonable intervals by secret ballot, under conditions which will ensure the free expression of the opinion of the people in the choice of the legislature.

After a period of unadventurous jurisprudence in the European Commission, the European Court of Human Rights concluded in *Mathieu-Morfin and Clerfayt* that the words of the Preamble were in fact of prime importance, since they enshrined 'a characteristic principle of

21   Art. 13: 1. 'Every citizen shall have the right to participate freely in the government of his country, either directly or through freely chosen representatives in accordance with the provisions of the law. 2. Every citizen shall have the right of equal access to the public service of his country. 3. Every individual shall have the right of access to public property and services in strict equality of all persons before the law.'

22   Art. 23: Right to Participate in Government: '1. Every citizen shall enjoy the following rights and opportunities: (a) to take part in the conduct of public affairs, directly or through freely chosen representatives; (b) to vote and to be elected in genuine periodic elections, which shall be by universal and equal suffrage and by secret ballot that guarantees the free expression of the will of the voters; and (c) to have access, under general conditions of equality, to the public service of his country. 2. The law may regulate the exercise of the rights and opportunities referred to in the preceding paragraph only on the basis of age, nationality, residence, language, education, civil and mental capacity, or sentencing by a competent court in criminal proceedings.' Art. 5 of the Charter of the Organization of American States declares the duty of members to promote the effective exercise of representative democracy; this has been reaffirmed in subsequent resolutions and also used as the basis for criticism of members considered to be in breach. See Franck, 'Democratic Governance,' 65-6.

23   See Goy, R., 'La garantie européenne du droit à de libres élections législatives: l'article 3 du premier protocole additionel à la Convention de Rome,' 5 *Revue de droit public* 1275 (1985), (hereafter, Goy, 'La garantie européenne du droit à de libres élections législatives'), for a fascinating and illuminating account of debates within the Consultative Assembly, the Committee of Ministers and related committees.

democracy'.[24] The Court further approved the progressive development in the thinking of the European Commission on Human Rights:[25]

> From the idea of an 'institutional' right to the holding of free elections...the Commission has moved to the concept of 'universal suffrage'...and then, as a consequence, to the concept of subjective rights of participation - the 'right to vote' and the 'right to stand for election to the legislature'...

The failure to express an *individual* right can nevertheless have serious implications from the perspective of enforcement. The key elements in article 3 are the words 'free', 'reasonable intervals', 'secret ballot', and 'free expression of the people'. It does not therefore prescribe any particular form or system for elections,[26] and does not exclude the freedom of States to qualify exercise of the right to vote or related freedoms, such as free expression of opinion under article 10 of the Convention,[27] provided 'the conditions do not curtail the rights in question to such an extent as to impair

---

24 Ser. A, No. 113, para. 47. See also J.G. Merrills, *The Development of International Law by the European Court of Human Rights*, (1988), 115-35; J.E.S. Fawcett, *The Application of the European Convention on Human Rights*, (2nd ed., 1987), 416-8.

25 Ser. A, No. 113, para. 51; see also Goy, 'La garantie européenne du droit à de libres élections législatives', 1311, 1314.

26 Although the principle of equality of treatment necessarily applies to Protocol 1, art. 3, the European Court considered that this does not imply 'that all votes must necessarily have equal weight as regards the outcome of the election or that all candidates must have equal chances of victory. Thus no electoral system can eliminate "wasted votes".' The Court also emphasized the relevance of context: 'any electoral system must be assessed in the light of the political evolution of the country concerned...features that would be unacceptable in the context of one system may accordingly be justified in the context of another..': ibid., para. 54. During drafting, both the United Kingdom and Belgian delegates were concerned to protect non-representative institutions in their parliaments, namely, the hereditary House of Lords and a nominated Senate. The European Commission has also observed that at the time of drafting, both majoritarian and proportional representation systems were part of the 'common heritage of political traditions' referred to in the Preamble; see Application 7140/75, *X v. United Kingdom*: 7 *Decisions and Reports* 95; Application 8765/79, *Liberal Party v. United Kingdom*: 21 *Decisions and Reports* 211.

27 In the *Handyside* case, the European Court referred to the 'demands of pluralism, tolerance and broadmindedness without which there is no "democratic society". This means...that every "formality", "condition", "restriction" or "penalty" imposed [in the sphere of art. 10] must be proportionate to the legitimate aim pursued': Ser. A., No. 24, para. 49. See also the *Lingens* case: Ser. A, No. 103; the freedom of the press is not just about conveying information, but also extends to comment and criticism of politicians; *Oberschlick v. Austria*, Case No. 6/1990/197/257, European Court of Human Rights, 23 May 1991.

their very existence and deprive them of their *effectiveness.*'[28]

The European system had to work its way towards recognizing the individual rights dimension in the electoral context. The 1966 Covenant on Civil and Political Rights, the OAS Convention and, to a lesser extent, the African Charter, made that clear from the start. As is shown below, the general principles relating to State responsibility in regard to elections are widely reflected in the practice of States throughout the world, and have been integrated in the supervision, observation and monitoring activities of the United Nations and non-governmental organizations. What also emerges is a picture of how the principle of effectiveness of obligations provides the means to accommodate cultural, historical and political variations within a process that remains formally committed to the objective of 'free and fair elections.'

2.4 United Nations Election Activities

UN human rights institutions are only now beginning to make progress in developing the political rights, but activities such as election monitoring and technical assistance at the field level are already contributing significantly to State practice, and thus also to the consolidation of norms and standards.

United Nations election activities can take a number of forms, ranging from the actual organization and conduct of elections, as in Cambodia, to the provision of technical assistance. The *Comprehensive Settlement Agreement* for Cambodia is an *international* agreement, which illustrates in broad strokes the minimum conditions considered by the international community as necessary for the conduct of free and fair elections. The goal of the civilian and military arrangements was, first, to establish a politically neutral and peaceful environment for elections to a constituent assembly,

---

28   Ibid., para. 52, emphasis added. Strictly speaking, in its earlier interpretations, art. 3 did not guarantee a right to vote. In Application 1065/61: 4 *Yearbook* 268, Belgian citizens resident in the Congo complained that they were denied participation in elections in Belgium. The Commission found their claim incompatible with the Convention, since the right to vote was not as such guaranteed: 'the Contracting States may...exclude certain categories of citizen, such...as overseas residents, from the vote, provided such exclusion does not prevent the free expression of the opinion of the people in the choice of the legislature.' Such limitations, however, must also be consistent with other provisions of the Convention. The way was thus open and in 1975, on applications from Belgium and the United Kingdom, the European Commission revised its approach, to hold that art. 3 did in fact give rise to an individual right to vote or to offer oneself as a candidate, which was necessarily implied by recognition of the principle of universal suffrage: see citations in Goy, 'La garantie européenne du droit à de libres élections législatives', 1314.

which in turn were a step towards the emergence of Cambodia as a country following 'a system of liberal democracy, on the basis of pluralism. It will provide for periodic and genuine elections... universal and equal suffrage... voting by secret ballot ... [and] a full and fair opportunity to organize and participate in the electoral process.'[29]

The *Agreement* provided that the election was to be held on a provincial basis, in accordance with a system of proportional representation and party lists. All Cambodians aged eighteen, including Cambodian refugees and displaced persons, were entitled to take part and to vote. Political parties could be formed by any group of five thousand registered voters, but party platforms had to be consistent with the principles and objectives of the *Agreement*. Voting was to be by secret ballot, with provision made for the disabled and those who could not read or write. At the campaign level, it was provided that 'the freedoms of speech, assembly and movement will be fully respected. All registered political parties will enjoy fair access to the media, including the press, television and radio.'[30] Further detail and practical guidance were provided in the Electoral Law and the Code of Conduct for Political Parties laid down by the United Nations. So far as the latter were the products of UN and individual expert contributions, their normative significance is nevertheless strengthened by their acceptance by Cambodia and in the international endorsement that followed the election and its results.[31]

The UN has also been engaged in *supervision*, for example, in Namibia, in a situation of decolonization in which all steps of the procedure, political and electoral, required 'certification'.[32] This included assessing the impartiality of the electoral authorities, freedom of organization and expression for political parties, political party observers at various stages of the electoral process, and fair access to the media, among others.

At the request of the government of a sovereign State, the UN may undertake *verification*; the electoral process is managed by a national agency, and the UN is asked to 'verify' the freedom and fairness of specifically defined aspects, or at different stages. The Secretary General

---

29   For text of the Comprehensive Settlement Agreement, see 31 *Int. Leg. Mat.* 180 (1992).

30   Comprehensive Settlement Agreement, Elections Annex (Annex 3): ibid.

31   See IPU, 'Report of IPU Election Observer Mission, Cambodia, 16 May-4 June 1993,' Geneva, (1993); *Bulletin de l'Assemblée Nationale,* (Paris), no. 7 du 8 juin 1993, 44.

32   See UN/UNDP: *Guidelines on Special Arrangements for Electoral Assistance,* (Aug. 1992); also Report of the Secretary General: UN doc. A/46/609, 19 Nov. 1991.

sent observers, for example, to monitor the work of the Supreme Electoral Council in Nicaragua in 1989, at the request of the government but also in the context of the Esquipulas II peace process.[33] Amongst other matters, the parties involved undertook to adopt measures guaranteeing the participation of political parties in the electoral process, to ensure free access to means of communication and to protect freedom of association and expression.

More controversial, so far as no international or peace process was involved, was the UN verification mission to Haiti to monitor the elections of December 1990. Besides observing political rallies and the balloting procedure, the UN also provided technical assistance in the form of information and civic education;[34] China, Cuba and Colombia opposed the UN's involvement in election monitoring in a sovereign State, arguing that it constituted a violation of article 2(7) of the UN Charter,[35] and many States continue to insist that there is *no* 'universal need for the United Nations to provide electoral assistance'.[36]

Such a high degree of UN involvement requires a specific mandate from the General Assembly, and election organization, supervision and even verification remain *exceptional* activities. United Nations guidelines also emphasize that before becoming involved, there should be a clear *international* dimension,[37] monitoring should cover the entire electoral process, geographical and chronological, from registration to election, there should be a specific request from the government and broad public support, and the electoral process should conform to the relevant principles of international human rights law, due account being taken of local customs

33 See Council of Freely Elected Heads of Government. *Observing Nicaragua's Elections, 1989-1990;* Garber and Gibson, *Electoral Assistance*, 19. The General Assembly approved the mission in UNGA res. 44/10, the first time the UN had monitored an election in a Member State; see also United Nations, *Establishment and Terms of Reference of the United Nations Observer Mission to Verify the Electoral Process in Nicaragua (ONUVEN)*: UN doc. A/44/375 (1989).

34 Garber & Gibson, *Electoral Assistance,* 19; Franck, 'Democratic Governance,' 72-4.

35 Franck rejects this argument, citing the opinion of the International Court of Justice on the issue of commitments binding a nation to electoral standards. The Court said that it could not 'discover, within the range of subjects open to international agreement, any obstacle or provision to hinder a State from making a commitment of this kind. A State, which is free to decide upon the principle and methods of popular consultation within its domestic order, is sovereign for the purpose of accepting a limitation of its sovereignty in this field. This is a conceivable situation for a State which is bound by institutional links to a confederation of States, or indeed to an international organization.' *Military and Paramilitary Activities in and against Nicaragua (Nicaragua v. United States of America)*, 1986 ICJ *Reports* 14, 141; cited in Franck, 'Democratic Governance,' at 81.

36 See, for example, UNGA res. 48/124, 20 Dec. 1993, para. 4.

37 Report of the Secretary-General, *Enhancing the effectiveness of the principle of periodic and genuine elections:* UN doc. A/46/609, 19 Nov. 1991, paras. 58, 79

and political practices.[38] Less extensive UN involvement may include the provision of support for international observation, 'follow and report' by a UN representative on the spot,[39] and the provision of electoral assistance, such as analysis, advice, equipment and training.[40] A continuing role for the UN in the democratization process is nevertheless clearly called for in the 1993 Vienna Declaration and Programme of Action:[41]

> Democracy, development and respect for human rights and fundamental freedoms are interdependent and mutually reinforcing...The international community should support the strengthening and promoting of democracy, development and respect for human rights and fundamental freedoms in the entire world.

2.4.1 Action in the UN General Assembly

In resolution 46/137, adopted on 18 December 1991 by 134 votes in favour, 4 against[42] and 13 abstentions, the UN General Assembly decided that the Secretary General should establish a focal point to ensure consistency in handling requests for electoral assistance, a post that was later to be assisted by the *Electoral Assistance Unit*, effective 1 April 1992.[43] That resolution reiterated the language of the basic principles set out above: the right of everyone to take part in the government of their country, directly or through freely chosen representatives, the right of equal access to public service, that the will of the people is the basis of the authority of government, and that this will shall be expressed in periodic and genuine elections, by

38   See UN/UNDP: *Guidelines on Special Arrangements for Electoral Assistance*, (Aug. 1992); *Guidelines for Member States Considering the Formulation of a Request for Electoral Assistance*, n.d.

39   'Follow and report' was initially employed where there was a perceived need for a United Nations presence, but insufficient lead time for a full operation. The UNDP Resident Representative was generally requested by the Secretary-General to assume 'follow and report' responsibilities. A recent review of UN election assistance activities has recommended that the practice be abandoned: Garber & Gibson, *Electoral Assistance*, 58.

40   The UN Centre for Human Rights, for example, provided analytical reports following missions to Albania in 1990, Romania in 1990 and 1992, Lesotho in 1991, and Malawi in 1993. In 1994, the Centre scheduled for publication a handbook on the legal, technical and human rights aspects of elections.

41   UN doc. A/CONF.157/23, paras. 8, 23.

42   Those voting against were Cuba, the Democratic People's Republic of Korea, Kenya and Namibia. Namibia later advised that it had intended to vote in favour. Already in 1988, in res. 43/157, 'Enhancing the effectiveness of the principle of periodic and genuine elections,' the General Assembly had invited the Commission on Human Rights to report on how the UN might support electoral processes while respecting the sovereignty of States.

43   See Report of the Secretary-General, *Enhancing the effectiveness of the principle of periodic and genuine elections*: UN doc. A/47/668, 18 Nov. 1992, paras. 9-12 on the role of the Unit.

universal and equal suffrage held by secret vote. Such elections are 'a necessary and indispensable element of sustained efforts to protect the rights and interests of the governed'; and 'determining the will of the people requires an electoral process that provides an equal opportunity for all citizens to become candidates and put forward their political views, individually and in co-operation with others...'

At the same time, the General Assembly recognized that there is no single political system or electoral method equally suited to all nations. Moreover, the efforts of the international community,

> to enhance the effectiveness of the principle of periodic and genuine elections should not call into question each State's sovereign right, in accordance with the will of its people, freely to choose and develop its political, social, economic and cultural systems, whether or not they conform to the preferences of other States

The 1992 and 1993 resolutions were both adopted without a contrary vote, each recognizing that 'the fundamental responsibility for ensuring free and fair elections lies with Governments'.[44]

Similar concerns have been reiterated in a series of 'parallel' resolutions, beginning with resolution 46/130 on 'Respect for the principles of national sovereignty and non-interference in the internal affairs of States in the electoral processes', adopted on 17 December 1991 by a vote of 102 in favour, 40 against and 13 abstentions;[45] it emphasized that 'electoral processes are subject to historical, political, cultural and religious factors,' a point reaffirmed in 1992 and 1993.[46]

The extent to which United Nations electoral activities have contributed to the consolidation of international norms and standards is considered below. A review of such activities published in August 1993 recommended that before any UN involvement takes place, a preliminary needs assessment mission should look at and review, among other matters, the viability of the election system, the potential for electoral manipulation, the specific

44   UNGA res. 47/138, 18 Dec. 1992 (Kenya joined those in favour); UNGA res. 48/131, 20 Dec. 1993 (Namibia joined those in favour).

45   Some of the concerns of States in favour of res. 46/130 are evident from operative para. 6, which 'Strongly appeals to all States to refrain from financing or providing, directly or indirectly, any other form of overt or covert support for political parties or groups and from taking actions to undermine the electoral processes in any country.'

46   See UNGA res. 48/124, 20 Dec. 1993; UNGA res. 47/130, 18 Dec. 1992.

requests for assistance from the government, the attitude of opposition parties to the UN or others providing assistance or monitoring, and the long-term significance of a successful election. Failure to engage in such a preliminary review could increase the likelihood of the UN becoming involved in a flawed process.[47] The General Assembly appears to agree; resolution 48/131 requests that the UN attempt 'to ensure, before undertaking to provide electoral assistance...that there is adequate time to organize and carry out an effective mission...that conditions exist to allow a free and fair election and that provisions can be made for adequate and comprehensive reporting of the results of the mission'. It also recommends that, 'in order to ensure the continuation and consolidation of the democratization process,' the UN should provide assistance both before and after elections.

2.5 The Inter-Parliamentary Union (IPU): Policy and Practice

The Inter-Parliamentary Union (IPU) has been the focus for worldwide parliamentary dialogue since its founding in 1889. Besides encouraging contacts among parliamentarians, the IPU also works to improve knowledge of representative institutions and to develop and strengthen their means of action. It collects and disseminates information, prepares comparative studies and provides technical assistance to Parliaments.

In a major study on *Electoral Systems*, published in 1993, the IPU set out its thinking on elections and the democratic process by emphasizing the necessity for a reasonable link between electors and elected in whichever system of balloting a State may choose, 'so as to avoid any possible divorce between the political class and the electorate.'[48] As the IPU Secretary General stated in his foreword, 'However fair and regular an election may be, its political outcome is evidently determined by the *electoral system* that is applied.' In reviewing the practice of some 150 countries, the IPU found that elections are usually carried out by direct universal suffrage, in which every citizen can vote unless disqualified by law. Most countries impose limitations with respect to nationality, age, and residence; at the time of the study, two States denied the franchise to a major proportion of their population, namely, blacks and women. There is also considerable variation

47   Garber & Gibson, *Electoral Assistance*, 58ff.

48   Inter-Parliamentary Union, *Electoral Systems: A World-Wide Comparative Survey*, Geneva, (1993). 3

among States in their choice of electoral system. The majoritarian approach still predominates, although different methods of proportional representation, as well as mixed systems, increasingly are being adopted. If the objective is to ensure that the elected parliament should reflect representative political forces as closely as possible, then minorities and special interest groups may need special attention; some countries achieve this through constituency delimitation, or by providing for the designation of minority or group members.

In the context of its commitment to the development and strengthening of representative institutions, the IPU is increasingly engaged in election monitoring, both in its own right and indirectly through parliamentarian members.[49] As part of its support to Parliaments, the 82nd Inter-Parliamentary Conference specifically endorsed the decision to send an IPU observer mission to 'verify the legality' of the elections in Namibia in 1989.[50] Its mandate on that occasion was to ascertain that all Namibians entitled to vote were properly registered and the rolls not tampered with; to observe whether all those registered were able to vote freely and that their ballots were properly and fairly counted; and to enquire whether, during the campaign and the election itself information flowed freely to and from the people so as to ensure that they were able to vote under the best possible conditions.[51]

Four years later the Inter-Parliamentary Council decided similarly to send a delegation to Cambodia, to observe all relevant aspects of the organization and conduct of the elections scheduled for May 1993, and to report on its observations and findings as to whether they were carried out in conformity with the UN Electoral Law for Cambodia.[52] The findings of both missions are incorporated in the body of the present study. As the IPU delegation to Cambodia emphasized, however, it is important not only that election observer missions witness the whole electoral process, including the campaign period, but also to recognize that 'elections are but part of a

49   Note that it was *parliamentarians* in the European Consultative Assembly who pushed for the inclusion of electoral rights in the European Convention on Human Rights; see Goy, 'La garantie européenne du droit à de libres élections législatives', 1278-90.

50   See Resolution on Support of Parliaments to the Process of Independence in Namibia, the Holding of Free and Equitable General Elections, and the Establishment of a New Government reflecting the Popular Will, adopted by the 82nd Inter-Parliamentary Conference, Sept. 1989. Annexed to 'Report of the Mission to Observe the Elections in Namibia': IPU doc. CL/146/10-R.1, 20 Dec. 1989.

51   IPU, 'Report of the Mission to Observe the Elections in Namibia,' para. 21.

52   IPU, 'Report of IPU Election Observer Mission, Cambodia, 16 May-4 June 1993,' Geneva, (1993).

larger process which aims at ensuring participatory democracy.'[53]

At its April 1993 session in New Delhi, the Inter-Parliamentary Council unanimously endorsed the Union's policy and involvement in electoral processes. It welcomed co-operation with the United Nations, reaffirming 'that the Union should always seek to ensure that it is present at national elections and referenda which are organized, supervised or verified' by the UN.[54] The Council further urged national groups to participate in election observer missions and to provide electoral assistance, while specifically welcoming plans to undertake the present study on free and fair elections.[55]

2.6 Regional and Other Developments

One of the most extensive and coherent statements of principle with respect to elections is found in the final document issued by the Conference on Security and Co-operation in Europe Meeting on the Human Dimension in Copenhagen in 1990.[56] The participating States recognized that pluralistic democracy and the rule of law are essential for ensuring respect for all human rights and fundamental freedoms. Among the 'elements of justice' essential to the full expression of the inherent dignity and of the equal and inalienable rights of all human beings are free elections held at reasonable intervals by secret ballot, government that is representative in character, in which the executive is accountable to the elected legislature or the electorate, and a clear separation between State and political parties. Section 7 of the Copenhagen Document is especially comprehensive, declaring that in order to ensure the will of the people serves as the basis of the authority of government, the participating States will,

- □ hold elections at reasonable intervals, as established by law;
- □ permit all seats in at least one chamber of the national legislature to be freely contested in a popular vote;
- □ guarantee universal and equal suffrage to adult citizens;
- □ ensure that votes are cast by secret ballot or by equivalent free voting procedure,[57] and that they are counted and reported

---

53   Ibid., paras. 61, 65.

54   'IPU's Policy and Involvement in Electoral Processes,' Resolution adopted unanimously by the Inter-Parliamentary Council at its 152nd Session, New Delhi, 17 Apr. 1993, paras. 1, 2.

55   Ibid., paras. 7, 8, 10.

56   CSCE: Document of the Copenhagen Meeting of the Conference on the Human Dimension: 29 June 1990: 29 I.L.M. 1305 (1990).

57   The reason for this throwback to the Universal Declaration of Human Rights is not at all clear.

honestly with the official results made public;

☐ respect the right of citizens to seek political or public office, individually or as representatives of political parties or organizations, without discrimination;

☐ respect the right of individuals and groups to establish, in full freedom, their own political parties or other political organizations and provide such political parties or other organizations with the necessary legal guarantees to enable them to compete with each other on a basis of equal treatment before the law and by the authorities;

☐ ensure that law and public policy work to permit political campaigning to be conducted in a fair and free atmosphere in which neither administrative action, violence nor intimidation bars the parties and the candidates from freely presenting their views and qualifications, or prevents the voters from learning and discussing them or from casting their vote free of fear of retribution;

☐ provide that no legal or administrative obstacle stands in the way of unimpeded access to the media on a non-discriminatory basis for all political groupings and individuals wishing to participate in the electoral process;

☐ ensure that candidates who obtain the necessary number of votes required by law are duly installed in office and are permitted to remain in office until their term expires or is otherwise brought to any end in a manner that is regulated by law in conformity with democratic parliamentary and constitutional procedures.

States also accepted the potential of national and foreign observers in enhancing the electoral process, stressed the importance of related 'political rights', and the value of co-operation and information exchange.[58] Although the CSCE process may fall short of the high normative character of an international treaty, co-operation has been the *leitmotif* of each meeting, the focus of which is increasingly detailed.[59] The fact that fifty-six States now participate in the process, many of them both adapting their laws to

---

58 Ibid., sections 8, 9, 22.

59 Principle IX of the Declaration on Principles Guiding Relations between Participating States, Helsinki Final Act, 1 Aug. 1975, declared: 'The participating States will develop their co-operation with one another and with all States in all fields in accordance with the purposes and principles of the United Nations...' Text in 1975 *Digest of United States Practice in International Law*, pp. 8, 10.

democratic ends and inviting international observers to attend their elections,[60] lends added weight to the standards emerging with respect to free and fair elections.

This conclusion is amply supported by the fact that similar 'normative' activities have also been undertaken by many other international actors in this field. Numerous election observation reports are quoted throughout this study, and the mainly non-governmental organizations responsible have contributed, at least indirectly, to clarifying norms through their recorded experience and recommendations. Inter-governmental organizations have also significantly increased their election-related activities. For its part, the Organization of American States adopted the 'agreement of Santiago on democracy and the renovation of the Inter-American System' in 1991, in which it declared its determination to 'strengthen representative democracy as the expression of the legitimate and free manifestation of popular will, in strict respect of the sovereignty and independence of its member States'.[61] This was followed by the establishment of an OAS Unit for the Promotion of Democracy and enhanced involvement in electoral assistance and observation.

Also in 1991, the Commonwealth adopted the Harare Declaration which gave high priority to the organization's promotion of its fundamental political values, defined as 'democracy, democratic processes and institutions which reflect national circumstances, human rights, the rule of law, and just and honest government'.[62] The Declaration has been followed by extensive activities for assisting and observing electoral processes. The Organization of African Unity has provided such assistance, observing, for example, the 1992 elections in Zambia. Most recently, and together with the Commonwealth and the European Union, the OAU has co-operated with the United Nations in observing the 1994 elections in South Africa.

---

60   Some 1,000 international observers are estimated to have attended the 12 Dec. 1993 elections in Russia: US Commission on Security and Cooperation in Europe. *Russia's Parliamentary Election and Constitutional Referendum, December 12, 1993.* Washington, D.C. (Jan. 1994), 13.
61   Resolution adopted at its third plenary session on 4 June 1991.
62   The Harare Commonwealth Declaration, October 1991.

3. FREE AND FAIR ELECTIONS

3.1 Constituent Elements

At a certain level of abstraction, States are bound to conduct their internal affairs, so that 'the authority to govern shall be based on the will of the people as expressed in periodic and genuine elections.' The principle of effectiveness of obligations requires that States adopt laws and procedures or systems of internal organization which are conducive to and do not obstruct the attainment of particular goals established by international law. This principle in turn carries certain implications with respect to the choice of options in regard to free and fair elections, even if none can be specifically framed as an international duty. These 'markers' for effective implementation, the indices for free and fair elections, are nonetheless evident in the practice of established democracies and States in transition, considered in relation to the attainment or failure to attain the stated objective. For the purposes of the present study, the requisite activities and criteria have been divided into the following ten broad categories: (1) Electoral law and system; (2) Constituency delimitation; (3) Election management; (4) The right to vote; (5) Voter registration; (6) Civic education and voter information; (7) Candidates, political parties and political organization, including funding; (8) Electoral campaigns, including protection and respect for fundamental human rights, political meetings, media access and coverage; (9) Balloting, monitoring and results; and (10) Complaints and dispute resolution.

3.1.1 Electoral law and system

Regional jurisprudence and recent United Nations General Assembly resolutions recognize 'that there is no single political system or electoral method that is equally suited to all nations and their people and that the efforts of the international community to enhance the effectiveness of the principle of periodic and genuine elections should not call into question each State's sovereign right, in accordance with the will of its people, freely to choose and develop its political, social, economic and cultural systems, whether or not they conform to the preferences of other States.'[1] Moreover, 'political systems and electoral processes are subject to historical, political,

---

1 See, for example, UNGA res. 46/137, 'Enhancing the effectiveness of the principle of periodic and genuine elections,' 17 Dec. 1991; also, UNGA res. 47/130, 18 Dec. 1992; UNGA res. 48/124, 20 Dec. 1993.

cultural and religious factors'.[2] Whether a State adopts a majoritarian voting system or one or other system of proportional representation is thus a classic issue falling within the reserved domain of domestic jurisdiction.[3]

State practice confirms the variety of available choices,[4] and no system can be considered, from an international law perspective, to be more valid than any other, provided it bears a reasonable relationship, in law and in practice, to the internationally prescribed objective. The IPU has noted the need, among others, to strike a balance between two essential considerations: that a legislative election above all must make it possible to designate a cohesive government responsible for conducting a national policy; and that the election primarily must guarantee representation at the national level of the country's political forces, and reproduce in Parliament as faithful an image as possible of their relative strength.[5] The IPU has also stressed the importance of a reasonable link between the electors and the elected, reflecting those elements of proportionality[6] which also characterize the governing principles of international law.

The chosen system, therefore, must facilitate the expression of the will of the people through periodic and genuine elections, conducted on the basis of equal suffrage and secret ballot. 'Periodic' is yet another of those terms susceptible to varying interpretations, even among reasonable people. The *travaux préparatoires* of article 3 of Protocol 1 to the European Convention on Human Rights find expert opinion saying that the intervals between elections should be neither too short nor too long, but rather in conformity with the normal practice of free States.[7] Practice in turn merely confirms the generality of the condition; random samples show that representatives in the United States of America serve two-year terms; Australia and New

2   UNGA res. 46/130, 'Respect for the principles of national sovereignty and non-interference in the internal affairs of States in their electoral processes,' 17 Dec. 1991.

3   See generally, Inter-Parliamentary Union, *Electoral Systems*, Geneva, (1993); Nadais, A., 'Choice of Electoral Systems,' in Garber, Larry and Bjornlund, Eric, eds., *The New Democratic Frontier. A country by country report on elections in Central and Eastern Europe*. National Democratic Institute for International Affairs, Washington, D.C., (1992), 190 (hereafter, Garber & Bjornlund, *New Democratic Frontier*).

4   See generally, Inter-Parliamentary Union, *Electoral Systems*, Geneva, (1993).

5   Ibid., 3.

6   'Proportionality' is used here and in similar contexts below in its international law sense of 'bearing a reasonable relationship between the means chosen and the required result'. On proportionality and non-discrimination, see Goodwin-Gill, G.S., *International Law and the Movement of Persons between States*, (1978), 75-82. In this sense, proportionality differs from and is not intended to be a substitute for elections systems based on 'proportional representation'.

7   Goy, 'La garantie européenne du droit à de libres élections législatives,' 1280.

Zealand, three years; Austria and Belgium, four years; Botswana and the United Kingdom, five years. The Inter-American Commission on Human Rights has ruled that the postponement of all elections for ten years violates the American Declaration of the Rights of Man,[8] thereby showing how the principle of proportionality can be applied in a specific situation.

Periodic and genuine elections conducted on the basis of equal suffrage also means 'equality of voting power'; in principle, no vote should carry disproportionately more weight than any other, but that does not *necessarily* require a system of proportional representation. On a complaint by a minority party member in the United Kingdom, the European Commission of Human Rights interpreted Protocol 1, article 3, to mean that different political parties must be given a reasonable opportunity to present their candidates for election, but did not require an electoral system which guaranteed that the total number of votes cast for each candidate or party be reflected in the composition of the legislature.[9]

The choice of electoral system and its implementation may nevertheless have a direct effect on related political rights. Majoritarian systems tend to favour two parties. They are relatively straightforward, but in a multi-party situation they give stability the advantage over equity in representation; not only are small or newer parties disadvantaged, but very large parliamentary majorities may be won on the basis of minor electoral victories, considered in percentage terms.[10] Proportional representation systems aim to allocate

8   Third Report on the Development of the Situation of Human Rights in Chile: doc. AR 1977, 77-99 (1977). Art. XX of the Declaration provides: 'Every person having legal capacity is entitled to participate in the government of his country, directly or through his representatives, and to take part in popular elections, which shall be by secret ballot, and shall be honest, periodic and free.'

9   Application 7140/75, 7 *Decisions and Reports* 95; cited in Sieghart, P., *The International Law of Human Rights*, (1983), 364 (hereafter, Sieghart, *Human Rights*.). See also Goy, 'La garantie européenne du droit à de libres élections législatives,' 1303-8 at 1306 (in a section pertinently entitled, 'L'absence de garantie d'une juste représentation').

10   IPU, *Electoral Systems*, 6. See also Council of Freely Elected Heads of Government and Carter Center of Emory University, *Electoral Reform in Mexico,* Occ. Paper Ser., Vol. IV, No. 1, Nov. 1993, 16-17 (hereafter Freely Elected Heads, *Electoral Reform in Mexico*).

seats to political parties proportional to their electoral strength; however, they can encourage the proliferation of parties, and require voting on the basis of party lists, so distancing the voter from the elected and in turn limiting the opportunities for individual, non-party candidatures.[11] Different formulae for the allocation of votes and seats can also significantly affect representation in the legislature, and may be adopted to ensure that no single party obtains a majority,[12] to maintain an urban-rural bias,[13] to ensure other 'balances',[14] or to guarantee minority or sectional

11   IPU, *Electoral Systems*, 7-8. AS the IPU study shows, mixed systems are also possible, the most comprehensive perhaps being those adopted in Germany and Hungary. In the 1990 Czechoslovak elections, parties might choose to include independent candidates on their list. The Bulgarian elections the same year featured a mixed majority and proportional representation system: US Commission on Security and Cooperation in Europe. *Elections in Central and Eastern Europe. A Compendium of Reports on the Elections Held from March through June 1990*. Washington, D.C., (July 1990), 127, 147 (hereafter US Commission, *Central and Eastern Europe 1990*). Elections in the Seychelles in July 1993 combined the majoritarian system for the presidency and two thirds of the legislature, and proportional representation for the remaining third: see *Bulletin de l'Assemblée Nationale*, no. 14 du 5 oct. 1993, 61. In Russia's 12 Dec. 1993 elections, half the 450 seats in the *duma* were assigned to single member constituencies decided on a simple majoritarian vote, and half were decided according to a system of proportional representation. See US Commission on Security and Cooperation in Europe. *Russia's Parliamentary Election and Constitutional Referendum, December 12, 1993*. Washington, D.C. (Jan. 1994), 7 (hereafter, US Commission, *Russia 1993*).

12   This appears to have been the stated aim of the voting system adopted for the Jordanian elections in Nov. 1993; cf. Antoine Boshard, 'Un résultat bien orchestré,' *Journal de Genève*, 10 nov. 1993, p. 3.

13   In Egypt, half of the 444 elected members must be labourers or farmers: Inter-Parliamentary Union, *Chronicle of Parliamentary Elections and Developments*, No. 25, 1990-1991, 65-6. See also Brick, A., Gastil, R. & Kimberling, W., *Mongolia: An Assessment of the Election to the Great People's Hural. June 1992*. International Foundation for Election Systems. Washington, D.C., (1992), 9, 17 (hereafter Brick, Gastil & Kimberling, *Mongolia 1992*). With respect to Zambia, see below note 26 and accompanying text.

14   In Tonga, for example, only nine of 30 seats in parliament are open to election by the country's 45,000 voters. Twelve seats are occupied permanently by the King and the 11-member Privy Council/Cabinet, and nine are reserved for and elected by the country's 'hereditary nobles': *Keesing's Record of World Events*, News Digest for February 1993. The House of Representatives in Fiji consists of 70 members elected for 5 years, of whom 37 are elected by voters on the Fijian communal roll, 27 by voters on the Indian communal roll, one by voters on the Rotuman communal roll and 5 by voters on the General communal roll: Inter-Parliamentary Union, *Chronicle of Parliamentary Elections and Developments*, No. 26, 1991-1992, 71.

representation.[15]

The principle of equal suffrage nevertheless applies also to 'threshold' requirements, which can be and are used to deny representation to parties that fail to secure a prescribed percentage of the overall vote.[16] Such criteria are commonly used to reduce the numbers of small or sectional interests in the legislature and to enhance the prospects for the formation of a viable government.[17] Unless compensatory steps are taken,[18] however, this technique can effectively disenfranchise substantial minorities. International standards nevertheless constrain and structure the choices available to States. The underlying obligation of result, combined with principles of equality, reasonableness and proportionality, can be used to mediate between the objective and the means chosen, and to show whether the system and its implementation in practice conform to what is required by international law. In short, the State is not free to use the 'valid' electoral technique of the threshold requirement in order to bar particular groups from representation in Parliament.

The choice of *system* reveals a wide disparity, or even richness, of practice. In many cases, the choice is not so much the result of conscious legislative decisions, as the product of a particular historical and political evolution. As such, it is not necessarily a model to be emulated out of context, although the representation aims of individual systems may appeal to countries in transition, where popular consensus on the democratic approach to government is still lacking. The general and distant objective set by international law — genuine periodic elections guaranteeing the free

---

15   In Iran, for example, Zoroastrians, Jews, Assyrian and Chaldean Christians and Armenian Christians of the South and North are all guaranteed one representative: Inter-Parliamentary Union, *Chronicle of Parliamentary Elections and Developments*, No. 26, 1991-1992, 83; in New Zealand, four of the 97 electoral districts are set aside for representatives of the Maori race (who make up 12% of the population): ibid., No. 25, 1990-1991, 111; the Cypriot constitution provides for power sharing between Greek and Turkish populations in proportion to their numbers: ibid., 57; both Bangladesh and Tanzania guarantee seats for women: ibid., 37, 123; in Lebanon, voters vote for lists which take count of the division of seats between the different religious communities: ibid., No. 27, 1992-1993, 135-8; in Croatia, ethnic and national minorities which constitute more than 8% of the population have a right to representation proportional to their numbers: ibid, 71-4; in Romania, legally constituted organizations of citizens belonging to a national minority which has not obtained at least one Deputy or Senator have the right to a Deputy's seat if they have obtained throughout the country at least 5% of the average number of validly expressed votes: ibid, 181-5.

16   The IPU *Electoral Systems* survey found thresholds ranging from 0.67 per cent in the Netherlands, to 8 per cent in Liechtenstein.

17   For example, the 5% threshold in Russia's 1993 elections was intended precisely to keep out small, 'troublesome' parties: US Commission, *Russia 1993*, 4.

18   Cf. the examples given in note 15 above.

expression of the will of the electors, which shall be the basis of the authority of the government — allows considerable room for variation. Whether an electoral system departs from the permissible range is most likely to be answered by reference to other peremptory international law principles, such as non-discrimination. Does the 'variation' have the intent or effect of disenfranchising or devaluing the voting power of particular sections of the population for reasons that ought to be irrelevant to the exercise of political rights, such as race, religion, national or social origin, sex, language, political or other opinion, association with a national minority, birth or other status? If so, then to that extent the electoral system is potentially in breach of international law.

3.1.2 Constituency delimitation

Constituency delimitation, or 'districting', raises similar considerations with respect to purpose, intent and effect, in an area of some flexibility. 'Representation by population' is as central to the concept of democracy as is the notion of equality of voting power; the question is whether absolute or near-absolute equality is called for; or whether relative equality of voting power will suffice. The United States Supreme Court, for example, held that the equal protection clause rendered unconstitutional a state districting scheme for congressional elections, because it failed to provide for equality of voters in each district;[19] in another instance, a disparity as small as 0.6984% was also held unconstitutional.[20]

Other States are more pragmatic, recognizing the importance of population, but also the relevance of other factors. A 1986 decision of the French *Conseil constitutionnel*, for example, confirmed constituency delimitation criteria which included the principle that population differences within a single *département* must not exceed 20% of the departmental average.[21] In the United Kingdom, Boundary Commissioners are required to draw constituency limits so as to come as close as possible to a regional average quota.[22] A Canadian decision in 1989 considered

19   *Reynolds v. Sims* (1964) 12 L.Ed.(2d) 506, 536; the disparity here was as high as 41-1, however.

20   *Karcher v. Daggett* (1983) 77 L.Ed.(2d) 133. Variations tend to be tolerated more at the level of state or local legislature; see *Mahon v. Howell* (1973) 34 L.Ed.(2d) 320; *Gaffney v. Cummings* (1973) 37 L.Ed.(2d) 298.

21   *Décision* no. 86-218, 16 nov. 1986.

22   European Centre for Parliamentary Research and Documentation, *Electoral System Legislation. National Reports: Part Two,* (May 1993), 473 (hereafter ECPRD, *Electoral System Legislation*). The quotas for 1992 were as follows: England-69,534; Scotland-54,570; Wales-58,383; Northern Ireland-67,145.

constituency deviations in British Columbia, which had the effect of enhancing the power of the rural vote. The Court considered that 'equality of voting power is the single most important factor to be considered in determining electoral boundaries,' but that 'relative equality of the number of voters per representative' was called for. The justifications put forward by the government on this occasion were held inadequate, however, and in some cases, 'it was difficult to see how they could conform to the principle that population must be the primary criterion.'[23] More recently, the Supreme Court of Canada has stressed that the purpose of the right to vote in section 3 of the *Charter* is not equality of voting power, so much as the right to 'effective representation', of which relative parity is a prime condition, but allows geography, community history, community interests and minority representation also to be taken into account.[24]

Few States follow the U.S. model of absolute equality, but seek instead to accord legislative seats roughly proportional to population. Boundary changes in Mongolia for the 1992 election, for example, reversed the rural bias of the 1990 elections.[25] 'Effective representation' was supposedly taken into account in creating additional constituencies for the October 1991 elections in Zambia, specifically for areas having severe physical and communication difficulties. When setting constituency boundaries, the Electoral Commission was required to take three criteria into account: the availability of means of communication; the geographical features of the area; and the number of inhabitants. It was authorised to vary the strict application of the population quota where either of the other criteria justified such action.[26] A clear rural bias resulted, together with substantial variations in voter numbers, ranging from 6,376 in one constituency, to 70,379 in

23   *Dixon v British Columbia (Attorney General)* [1989] W.W.R. 393. In one example, the constituency of Atlin had 2,420 voters, while another, Coquitlam-Moody, had 36,318, making a vote in the former 15 times more valuable than a vote in the latter: 'Such anomalies cannot but suggest a gross violation of the fundamental concept of representation by population which is the foundation of our political system.'

24   *Reference Re Provincial Electoral Boundaries (Saskatchewan)* [1991] S.C.J. No. 46. See the decision to similar effect of the Australian High Court in *Attorney-General of the Commonwealth (ex rel. McKinlay) v. Commonwealth of Australia* (1975) 135 C.L.R. 1.

25   Brick, Gastil & Kimberling, *Mongolia 1992*, 17. The deviation from the norm of some 13,000 voters per seat was plus or minus some 2,500, ranging from a high of some 16,000 to a low of some 11,000. Although unacceptable in the United States, 'it is not unreasonable in the demography of Mongolia - especially considering that they tried to respect traditional political boundaries': ibid.

26   Commonwealth Secretariat, *Presidential and National Assembly Elections in Zambia, 31 October 1991.* Report of the Commonwealth Observer Group, (1992), 4 (hereafter Commonwealth Observer Group, *Zambia 1992*).

another.[27] Even though all parties accepted the delimitation, such substantial variations inevitably devalued many votes.

While the principle of relative equality will ensure that votes carry more or less equal value, subject to objectively justifiable variations on the basis of local or regional conditions, clearly no rule prescribes the ideal ratio of population to representative. The International Foundation for Electoral Systems in its pre-electoral evaluation in Togo (estimated total population, 3.6 million; estimated total electorate, 1.7 million), considered that a ratio of 1:25,000 meant weak representation.[28] Much will depend on local conditions, however; voting districts for the Latvian elections in 1990 were tied to approximately 10,000 voters, those in Lithuania under the October 1989 laws to some 18,400;[29] the rule in Ireland is at least one member for every 30,000 inhabitants, and not more than 1 for every 20,000;[30] the representation norm for Romania in the September 1992 elections was one deputy for every 70,000 inhabitants, while average constituency size in Bangladesh for the 1991 parliamentary elections was 207,631,[31] and each of China's 2,978 indirectly elected deputies represented approximately 335,000 inhabitants.[32] The level of representation will depend not only on population and geography, but also on overall political organization. For example, federal States with functioning and effective provincial legislatures, or unitary States with highly developed systems of local

27   National Democratic Institute for International Affairs. Carter Center of Emory University. *The October 31 1991 National Elections in Zambia*. Washington, D.C., (1992), 32-3 (hereafter NDI/Carter Center, *Zambia 1991*)

28   Brunet, G., Marchand, M., et Neher, L., *Togo: Rapport d'évaluation pré-électorale*. International Foundation for Election Systems, (31 mars 1992), 21 (hereafter Brunet, Marchand & Neher, *Togo 1992*). As the Canadian Court noted in *Dixon* (above note 23), 'It is not consistent with good government that one member be grossly overburdened with constituents, as compared with another member.'

29   US Commission on Security and Cooperation in Europe. *Elections in the Baltic States and Soviet Republics*. A Compendium of Reports on Parliamentary Elections Held in 1990. Washington, D.C., (Dec. 1990), 22, 64.

30   ECPRD, *Electoral System Legislation,* 302.

31   Commonwealth Secretariat, *Parliamentary Elections in Bangladesh, 27 February 1991*. Report of the Commonwealth Observer Group, (1991), 11 (hereafter, Commonwealth Observer Group, *Bangladesh 1991*). The boundaries had been drawn in 1984, on the basis of the 1981 census, again so as to achieve broad equality of voters among constituencies and satisfaction of other criteria. Given the substantial interim changes, particularly due to population movements, the Commonwealth Observer Group recommended review.

32   Inter-Parliamentary Union, *Chronicle of Parliamentary Elections and Developments*, No. 27, 1992-1993, 59-61. The law in the Dominican Republic provides for one deputy for every 50,000 inhabitants or fraction thereof greater than 25,000: ibid., No. 24, 1989-1990, 67. In Mexico, the ratio is one deputy for every 250,000 citizens, and for every fraction over 125,000: ibid., No. 26, 1991-1992, 113.

government, may satisfy international standards with a relatively low ratio of representation to population.

From an international law perspective, how a State delimits its electoral boundaries remains very much a product of its overall choice of electoral system. The general aim remains the same, to translate the will of the people into *representative* government. Again, State practice and the very disparities between States themselves in terms of population, geography, distribution and resources, reveal the range of possible and permissible variations. Substantial differences in the representation/population ratio between electoral units, however, raise a number of questions. For example, does the disparity have the effect of disenfranchising a group or groups of the population, contrary to the international norm of non-discrimination? Or does the unequal division have a political impact, in the sense of affecting the outcome of an election? Either case raises the possibility of a violation of international law, although a breach will normally be determined only by what actually happens in fact.

3.1.3 Election management

In a free and fair election, an independent and impartially administered electoral process is essential. Mexican observers of the United States system in 1992 remarked on the absence of government and parties from the process, and on the degree of decentralization. They also noted the degree of *trust* in the system, which they attributed to a combination of history, active media, fear of publicity, and effective judicial remedies.[33] Countries in transition frequently also suffer a lack of trust among the political players; 'for a democratic election to occur, all major parties...must accept the process and respect the results.[34]' Experience shows that confidence is only likely where the election machinery is and appears to be impartial.[35]

Frequently, and particularly in established democracies, administration is handled by national and local government officials and disputes are settled by ordinary courts having a tradition of fairness and neutrality, all of whom enjoy the confidence of the electorate on that account alone. In France, for example, the local *bureau de vote* comprises a president,

33   Freely Elected Heads, *Electoral Reform in Mexico*, 11.
34   Ibid., 8. Trust was the key element in the successful transfer of power in Nicaragua in 1990. All political parties undertook to accept the results, both before and after the election: Council of Freely Elected Heads of Government. *Observing Nicaragua's Elections, 1989-1990*, 25-6.
35   Cf. Council of Freely Elected Heads of Government. *Observing Guyana's Electoral Process 1990-1992* (1992).

generally the mayor, deputy mayor or a municipal counsellor, and four assessors and a secretary, chosen from among the electors of the commune.[36] Local electoral committees in Norway are drawn from municipal executive boards;[37] those in Sweden are appointed by the municipal council;[38] the electoral registration officials in England and Wales are either the chief executive officers or other senior officers of local government authorities, while the returning officer responsible for administering the election will again be a senior local official, with election staff usually local government employees on temporary transfer.[39]

In very exceptional cases, such as occurred in Bangladesh in 1991,[40] the responsibility for an election may be conferred on a caretaker government having no commitment to any particular political party. In other situations of transition, either from conflict to peace or from a single-party to a multi-party system, positive steps will be required to generate a credible electoral process and instill the necessary confidence in all the parties.

At a practical administrative and oversight level, the institution of an independent *Electoral Commission* is now widely adopted as an important step in building traditions of independence and impartiality, and the confidence of the electorate and parties alike. Eastern European countries, including Hungary, Slovenia, Romania, Poland, Czechoslovakia and Bulgaria all established central commissions for the crucial elections of 1989-90.[41] Different systems were employed, including commissions made up of an equal number of representatives of parties contesting the election; party commissions with the addition of government-selected members; party representatives in proportion to the numbers of candidates fielded, plus a number of judges or jurists selected by lot; and commissions with members designated by parties involved in pre-election negotiations.[42]

In practice, the election machinery can either be impartial, or in balance;

---

36   Masclet, Jean-Claude, *Droit électoral*, 277-81; ECPRD, *Electoral System Legislation,* 250.
37   ECPRD, *Electoral System Legislation,* 342-3.
38   Ibid., 428.
39   Ibid., 471, 473.
40   Commonwealth Observer Group, *Bangladesh 1991*, 6, 28. As the Group observed, 'From this reality has flowed a neutral administration and an Election Commission ... with full command of all election staff and security personnel; an atmosphere palpably free and peaceful in the polling stations; confidence and enthusiasm among voters and candidates alike; and a campaign which was open and for the most part even exuberant.'
41   Nadais, A., 'Choice of Electoral Systems,' in Garber & Bjornlund, *New Democratic Frontier*, at 190, 197-8.
42   Ibid., at 198.

if impartial members who enjoy the confidence of all parties cannot be found, then balance must be created by the appointment of party representatives. In East Germany, election administration for the re-unification vote was handled by the forty-eight member National Election Commission, comprising two representatives from each of the twenty-four parties on the ballot; below it were district and local election commissions. The institution of an electoral commission was not new, but its commitment to free elections was. It rapidly established a reputation as fully independent and non-partisan, enjoyed ready access to the media, which it used in the interests of voter education, and supervised the reporting of both preliminary and final results.[43] In Hungary, four levels of election committee operated: national, county, constituency and polling place. Their membership comprised three non-party members appointed either by the national legislature or municipal council, together with representatives from each party with a candidate standing in the jurisdiction. The process was reported as having worked smoothly, and all parties appeared to trust the integrity of the election officials.[44] Bulgaria's twenty-four member Central Election Commission was headed by a well-respected law professor, not affiliated with any party. Three parties each designated one of the other three principal officers, and apportioned the 20 remaining seats among themselves.[45] The electoral law in Romania provided that the Central Electoral Bureau administer the elections, with authority delegated to provincial electoral bureaux. Both levels were composed of judges and party representatives, but the latter came in late. The political independence of the judges was doubtful, although the partiality of the bureaux finally was not a major issue.[46] In complete contrast was the situation in Czechoslovakia, where the Communist Party was already out of power and election administration fell to a coalition of dissidents whose commitment

---

43   Gordon, D. & Reinke, F., 'East Germany,' in Garber & Bjornlund, *New Democratic Frontier*, at 32-4.
44   Melia, T.O., 'Hungary', in Garber & Bjornlund, *New Democratic Frontier*, at 58.
45   Garber, L., 'Bulgaria,' in Garber & Bjornlund, *New Democratic Frontier*, at 141.
46   Carothers, T., 'Romania,' in Garber & Bjornlund, *New Democratic Frontier*, at 81. Of greater concern in the 1990 elections was the total absence of 'civil structures external and parallel to government'. This 'proved devastating to the inculcation of a free democratic process...A lack of civic education compounded the absence of civil society.' Ibid., at 87-8. See also concerns expressed by the Council of Europe delegation to Lithuania in October and November 1992: CE Doc. 6724, Add. II, para. 5.3 (20 Jan. 1993).

to free and fair election inspired public confidence.[47]

Perhaps the most striking exercise in confidence-building occurred in South Africa, where the government appointed several international members of the Independent Electoral Commission, including individuals from Canada, Zimbabwe and Eritrea.[48]

The ideal or most effective model will depend on the relative maturity of the national system. Where election administration previously was in government hands within a one-party or other authoritarian system with no opposition, voter confidence will only likely be inspired if opposition party representatives are co-opted into election administration. They may not be 'independent', and indeed will usually remain partisan, though ideally in balance with competing interests; at such moments, the issue is not so much *independence* as transparency and non-governmental involvement at national and polling district levels.[49] Later, when other government institutions acquire a reputation for impartiality and integrity, for example, when judges are seen to stand for the rule of law and not the party line, then independence alone may be a credible criterion for electoral commission membership.

The practical value of *dialogue* and *consultation* is reiterated in numerous observer reports, particularly in situations of transition. Recent analysis of electoral reform moves in Mexico found that the political parties

47 Carnahan, R. & Corley, J., 'Czechoslovakia', in Garber & Bjornlund, *New Democratic Frontier*, at 133.

48 Independent Electoral Commission Act, s.5(2).

49 This is not to say that the independence and impartiality of Commission members, particularly the Chair, are irrelevant. The Commonwealth Observer Group to the 1992 Kenya elections, for example, called attention to the 'regrettable circumstances' attaching to the appointment of the Chairman of the Electoral Commission, whose integrity was in doubt: Commonwealth Secretariat, *The Presidential, Parliamentary and Civil Elections in Kenya, 29 December 1992*. Report of the Commonwealth Observer Group, (1993), 9-11 (hereafter, Commonwealth Observer Group, *Kenya 1992*). Similarly, the report on the 1992 Ghana elections regretted that the Interim National Electoral Commission had been established and filled without consultation, let alone agreement of the parties: Commonwealth Secretariat, *The Presidential Election in Ghana, 3 November 1992*, Report of the Commonwealth Observer Group, (1992), 40-2 (hereafter Commonwealth Observer Group, *Ghana 1992*). In both cases, the institutions were able slowly to secure recognition of their impartiality. Commonwealth Observer Groups have emphasized that Electoral Commissions should not only be independent, but should be perceived as such. In Malaysia, the Group recommended that the Electoral Commission should report both to Government and to Parliament: Commonwealth Secretariat, *General Elections in Malaysia, 20-21 October 1990*. Report of the Commonwealth Observer Group, n.d., 4 (hereafter Commonwealth Observer Group, *Malaysia 1990*); also Commonwealth Observer Group, *Kenya 1992*, 10-11. It has been suggested that partiality in the election machinery can be compensated by the presence of international observers, *if* they are allowed: Freely Elected Heads, *Electoral Reform in Mexico*, 32.

have difficulty communicating with each other.[50] The Commonwealth Observer Group to the 1992 Kenya elections regretted the Government's inability to entertain any dialogue with the new opposition parties.[51] The need to 'institutionalize' the process of dialogue, even informally, was also emphasized after the 1992 Ghana elections.[52]

Poland's 1991 election law makes particularly detailed provision for election commissions, at the national, constituency and polling district level.[53] The National Election Commission is described as 'a permanent organ vested with the authority to deal with preparation, organization and conduct of the elections'.[54] It is composed of three judges each of the Supreme Court, the Constitutional Tribunal and the High Administrative Court, recommended respectively by the President of each Court and appointed by the President of the Republic of Poland.[55] A National Election Office is also established, among other things, to provide secretariat services and advice to the National Election Commission.[56] No person who is a member of a commission may stand as a candidate, act as a party agent or poll watcher, or engage in political canvassing.[57]

The National Election Commission's duties, to be performed directly or by supervision over the lower echelons, include supervising observance of the election law; organizing the preparation and conduct of elections; appointing constituency election commissions; examining complaints against constituency election commissions; registering national lists of candidates; compiling and supervising the updating of voter registries; keeping constituency delimitation under review; establishing forms and standards for ballot paper and other official documents; establishing and publishing the definitive results of elections; certifying those who are

50   Freely Elected Heads, *Electoral Reform in Mexico*, 32.

51   Commonwealth Observer Group, *Kenya 1992*, vii, 9-10,

52   Commonwealth Observer Group, *Ghana 1992*, 62-3. Reference was made to the Election Council established for the 1980 independence elections in Zimbabwe: 'This served not only as a forum in which parties could air grievances but also as a useful gathering in which those responsible for the election could consult with parties and inform them of recent developments. It had no executive role and its usefulness lay in its function as a sounding-board.'

53   Act of 28 June 1991 on election to the *Sejm* of the Republic of Poland, Ch. 6, Election Commissions, art. 44.

54   Ibid., art. 48.

55   Ibid., art. 53. Constituency election commissions are also composed of judges (art. 57), while polling district commissions are appointed by the municipal council from among voters, taking account of proposals by electoral committees (art. 61).

56   Ibid., art. 55.

57   Ibid., art. 45.

elected; and reporting to the *Sejm* on the conduct of elections.[58]

The value of independent election commissions is evident in the reports of a succession of observation missions, such as those of the Commonwealth Observer Groups cited above, even as individual commissions failed to fulfil their promise. The Central Election Commission of Mongolia, for example, seems to have exercised too little authority in the June 1992 elections, in contrast to the District Electoral Commissions. The membership of the latter caused concern, however, since nearly every Chair and Secretary was a member of the ruling party. Given the many and various responsibilities, the opportunities for fraud and unspoken voter intimidation were considerable. The IFES made a number of recommendations designed to enhance the independence and credibility of the Commissions.[59]

In its 1992 pre-election evaluation of Togo, IFES recommended the creation of an objective, non-partisan national electoral commission, given the history of one-party rule.[60] The National Democratic Institute's review of the 1992 election in Cameroon doubted the value of ministerial administration of elections, particularly where every 'divisional and senior divisional officer had to be personally approved by the president, who was, of course, contesting the election.[61]' An observer mission to the Dominican Republic in 1990 found the political parties also distrusting the Central Electoral Board.[62] Similar, though anticipatory concerns, were expressed in NDI's assessment of the Senegalese electoral code in 1991. It recommended greater participation by opposition parties in monitoring the administration of national elections.[63] This was generally accepted, although at the 1993 Presidential elections the National Vote Tabulation Commission, which included a representative designated by each party, was

58   Ibid., art. 49; see art. 56 for the duties of the constituency election commission, and art. 60 for the duties of the polling district election commission. Compare the responsibilities of the Interim National Electoral Commission in the 1992 Ghana elections: Commonwealth Observer Group, *Ghana 1992*, 6.

59   Brick, Gastil & Kimberling, *Mongolia 1992*, 13-14.

60   Brunet, Marchand & Neher, *Togo 1992*, 37.

61   National Democratic Institute for International Affairs. *An Assessment of the October 11, 1992 Election in Cameroon*. Washington, D.C., (1993), 18-20, 52, 54 (hereafter NDI, *Cameroon 1992*)

62 .   Council of Freely Elected Heads of Government. National Democratic Institute for International Affairs. *1990 Elections in the Dominican Republic: Report of an Observer Delegation*. Special Report #2, (1990), 20.

63   National Democratic Institute for International Affairs. *An Assessment of the Senegalese Electoral Code*. International Delegation Report. Washington, D.C., (1991), 24-6, 44 (hereafter NDI, *Senegal 1991*)

unable to accomplish its task because of partisan divisions among its members.[64]

IFES also expressed concern in 1992 at the absence of any permanent Central Election Commission or Central Election Bureau in Romania, which in turn resulted in the lack of guidelines and adequate training for election officials.[65] A report on the 1990 elections noted the 'passive stance' of local electoral commissions, most of which were headed by former Communist party election organizers. In many locations the integrity of the electoral process was severely compromised, both by the absence of opposition party representatives at polling sites and by active intimidation.[66] Considerable improvements were noted at the time of the 1992 elections, however.[67]

The positive role to be played by electoral commissions in difficult or transition situations was reported in respect to the 1990 elections in Bulgaria,[68] the 1991 parliamentary elections in Bangladesh,[69] and (after a shaky start) the 1992 presidential election in Ghana.[70] The generally receptive governmental response to UN recommendations for an independent referendum commission in Malawi in 1993 also contributed to the overall success of the vote.[71]

The consolidation of democracy requires that the institution that manages the electoral process be independent, competent, and perceived as

---

64   National Democratic Institute for International Affairs. 'Executive Summary. February 21, 1993 Presidential Elections in Senegal.' International Delegation Report. Washington, D.C. (1993).

65   Atwood, S.J., Villaveces, M.M., *IFES Technical Election Assistance Project, Romania, March 10-September 29. 1992. Report*. International Foundation for Election Systems. Washington, D.C., (1992). See also National Democratic Institute for International Affairs. *The October 1990 Elections in Pakistan*. Report of the International Delegation. Washington, D.C., (1991), 28-9, 54-5, 112-3 (hereafter NDI, *Pakistan 1990*).

66   US Commission on Security and Cooperation in Europe. *Elections in Central and Eastern Europe*. A Compendium of Reports on the Elections Held from March through June 1990. Washington, D.C., (Jul. 1990), 95, 97, 109, 112-3.

67   Atwood, S.J., Villaveces, M.M., *IFES Technical Election Assistance Project, Romania, March 10-September 29. 1992. Report*, 15.

68   National Democratic Institute for International Affairs. National Republican Institute for International Affairs. *The June 1990 Elections in Bulgaria*. International Delegation Report. Washington, D.C., (1990), 24 (hereafter NDI/NRI, *Bulgaria 1990*).

69   Above, text to note 40.

70   Commonwealth Observer Group, *Ghana 1992*, 40-2.

71   *Report of the Joint International Observer Group on the Malawi National Referendum*, 14 Jun. 1993 (hereafter JIOG, *Malawi 1993*). Both the Nov. 1992 preliminary mission and the UN Centre for Human Rights report in Jan. 1993 recommended a commission independent of the government; additional opposition members were appointed by the government.

completely fair by all the candidates and parties participating in the process.[72]

These objectives may not be established all at once, however, in which case experience shows that confidence in an emergent multi-party system is only likely if the parties themselves are co-opted into the process of election management. The practices described above illustrate the alternatives, which derive not so much from legal obligation, as from good management sense.

The centrality of impartial and trustworthy election machinery is often taken for granted in established democracies. Few go so far as Costa Rica, for example, which has established its election commission as the 'Fourth Branch' of government, with funding and terms of membership guaranteed by the constitution. Whether explicitly or implicitly endorsed, independent and impartial election management is nevertheless essential in the transition to and consolidation of representative democracy.

3.1.4 The right to vote

Formal constitutional or statutory recognition of the citizen's right to vote is common to most States and plays both a substantive and a confidence-building role; a few countries make voting compulsory.[73] The right to vote is not absolute, however, and may be subject to reasonable restrictions which 'are not arbitrary and do not interfere with the free expression of the people's opinion'.[74] With respect to parliamentary elections, most States lay down citizenship, age and residency requirements. In its recent world-wide comparative survey, the IPU noted that 18 years is currently the voting age norm, adopted by some 109 States

72   Council of Freely Elected Heads of Government. National Democratic Institute for International Affairs. *1990 Elections in the Dominican Republic: Report of an Observer Delegation.* Special Report #2, (1990), 20.

73   A cursory review of secondary sources for the last four years found only 16 countries with compulsory voting at one or other level: France (by the Electoral College for the Senate only); Nauru; Peru (until age 70): Inter-Parliamentary Union, *Chronicle of Parliamentary Elections and Developments,* No. 27, 1992-1993, 85, 163, 177; Argentina; Belgium; Ecuador; Italy; Philippines; Singapore; Turkey: Inter-Parliamentary Union, *Chronicle of Parliamentary Elections and Developments,* No. 26, 1991-1992, 37, 41, 67, 91, 113, 123, 145, 165; Egypt (compulsory for men): Inter-Parliamentary Union, *Chronicle of Parliamentary Elections and Developments,* No. 25, 1990-1991, 65; Australia; Costa Rica; Democratic People's Republic of Korea; Dominican Republic; Greece (for those under 70): Inter-Parliamentary Union, *Chronicle of Parliamentary Elections and Developments,* No. 24, 1989-1990, 29, 53, 61, 67, 81.

74   Sieghart, *Human Rights,* 363.

of the 150 surveyed.[75] A residency requirement has been upheld by the European Commission on Human Rights, for a number of reasons: the assumption that a non-resident citizen is less directly involved or knowledgeable; the impracticability for candidates to present electoral issues to citizens abroad; the need to prevent electoral fraud, the risk of which is increased by postal voting; and finally, the link between representation and the obligation to pay taxes.[76] In practice, however, there is a growing tendency to *broaden* the franchise, for example, by including overseas residents. A 1990 amendment to Austria's electoral law provides that every citizen living abroad may vote, whether he or she has a residence in the country or not.[77] The concept of citizenship is also expanding at regional level; the Maastricht Treaty, for example, establishes both a 'citizenship' of the European Union, and the right to vote and to stand for election to municipal bodies in the Member State where such citizen resides, on the same terms as local citizens.[78] To similar effect, the Council of Europe's 1992 Convention on the Participation of Foreigners in Public Life at Local Level also aims to extend the right to vote and to stand in local authority elections to foreign residents.[79]

The rule of law requires that the classes of those disqualified from voting, if any, be known in advance, and that challenge be available in appropriate cases. Section 3 of the Canadian *Charter of Rights and Freedoms,* for example, guarantees all citizens the right to vote, while section 15 establishes equality before the law. The *Canada Elections Act* excludes certain categories, but the courts have declared that

75   IPU, *Electoral Systems*, 4. Art. 1 of the 1989 United Nations Convention on the Rights of the Child defines a child to mean 'every human being below the age of 18 years unless, under the law applicable to the child, majority is attained earlier'. See also art. 1, 1990 African Charter on the Rights and Welfare of the Child, to similar effect.

76   Application 7566/76, 9 *Decisions and Reports* 121; cited in Sieghart, *Human Rights*, 363.

77   Inter-Parliamentary Union, *Chronicle of Parliamentary Elections and Developments*, No. 25, 1990-1991, 33.

78   See Maastricht Treaty, Title 1, Article F; Part Two (Citizenship of the Union), Articles 8, 8b. The European citizen is also entitled to vote and stand as candidate for the European Parliament in his or her Member State country of residence: art. 8b(2).

79   Council of Europe, 1992 Convention on the Participation of Foreigners in Public Life at Local Level: ETS No. 144, art. 6. Freedom of expression, peaceful assembly and association are also protected: art. 3. As the former carries with it 'duties and responsibilities', it may be subject to such formalities, conditions, restrictions or penalties as are prescribed by law and are necessary in a democratic soceity, in the interests of national security, territorial integrity or public safety, for the protection of health or morals, for the protection of the reputation or rights of others, for preventing the disclosure of information received in confidence, or for maintaining the authority and impartiality of the judiciary': art. 9(2). The freedoms of peaceful assembly and association may also be restricted, though to a lesser degree: art. 9(3).

federally-appointed judges and the mentally handicapped are constitutionally entitled to vote. In a 1993 judgment the Supreme Court of Canada also ruled that the statutory exclusion of prison inmates was drawn too broadly and failed to meet the proportionality test.[80] On the other hand, in another 1993 decision, the Supreme Court ruled that the *Charter* does not guarantee Canadians a constitutional right to vote in a *referendum*, 'basically a consultative process', as opposed to elections of representatives of the federal and provincial legislative assemblies.[81] Those who, by reason of residence requirements, were unable to vote in a referendum, were beyond the scope of the constitutionally protected equality provision.[82]

Other countries likewise maintain residency requirements as a basic condition of entitlement to vote,[83] but tend to be equally or more restrictive with respect to those suffering from mental disability or convicted of criminal offences.[84] Some countries also disqualify military personnel from

80   *Sauvé v. Canada (Attorney General)* [1993] 2 SCR 438.
81   The European Commission on Human Rights reached a similar conclusion with respect to the United Kingdom's referendum on European Community membership: Application 7096/75: 3 *Decisions and Reports* 165; cited in Sieghart, *Human Rights*, 365; Goy, 'La garantie européenne du droit à de libres élections législatives,' 1290-7.
82   Cf. the interpretation of art. 3, Protocol 1, European Convention on Human Rights, in Application 1065/61: above, note 28. Also, Schweizer, R., 'Zur Stellung der Schweiz gegenüber Art. 3 des Zusatzprotokolls zur Europäischer Menschenrechtskonvention (Gewährleistung von freien under geheimen Wahlen),' 41, 43-4.
83   Cf. art. 50, Constitution of the Kingdom of Norway 1814, as amended 10 June 1988: the extent to which those resident abroad or suffering from a seriously weakened mental state may be entitled to vote shall be determined by law; art. 6, Act of 28 June 1991 on election to the *Sejm* of the Republic of Poland: citizens aged 18 may vote, as may those whose Polish citizenship has not been ascertained, who are not citizens of another country, and have been resident for five years. Citizenship, age 18 and residence were common requirements for voting in the 1990 elections in various East European countries, including the German Democratic Republic, Slovenia, Croatia, and Romania; Czechoslovakia and Bulgaria both allowed non-resident citizens to return to vote. See US Commission, *Central and Eastern Europe 1990*, at 14, 65, 79, 107, 127, 153. Exclusions on mental health grounds were common to the electoral laws of the same countries. See also Senegal (citizenship, age 21 and 6 months residency, though with provision for registration of citizens residing overseas): NDI, *Senegal 1991*, 12); Pakistan (citizenship, age 21, 'deemed' to be a resident of the electoral district): NDI, *Pakistan 1990*, 32.
84   Cf. art. 53, Constitution of the Kingdom of Norway 1814, as amended 10 June 1988: the right to vote is lost by persons sentenced for criminal offences; also art. 7, Act of 28 June 1991 on election to the *Sejm* of the Republic of Poland. Those serving prison sentences were excluded in the German Democratic Republic, Hungary, and Bulgaria; Czechoslovakia allowed prisoners to vote in the locality where they were incarcerated. See US Commission, *Central and Eastern Europe 1990*, at 14, 127, 147. See also Senegal (exclusion of those convicted): NDI, *Senegal 1991*, 12; Cameroon (exclusion of those convicted of felony): NDI, *Cameroon 1992*, 21. Restrictions on prisoners' right to vote have been upheld by the European Commission on Human Rights; see Applications 2728/66: 25 *Collection of Decisions* 38; 4984/71: 43 *Collection of Decisions* 28.

voting, a practice particularly common in Latin America.[85] Such limitations, provided they have a rational basis, remain proportional and are not used as a device to disenfranchise significant sections of the population, arguably fall with the margin of appreciation left to States. Discriminatory disenfranchisement, however, would violate general principles of international law.

The United Nations Human Rights Committee (HRC) has considered the principles of equality and non-discrimination in relation to access to public service under article 25 of the 1966 Covenant on Civil and Political Rights. In *Silva and Others v. Uruguay*, the applicants claimed violation of their article 25 rights, so far as they had been deprived by law of the right to engage in political activity, including the right to vote, for fifteen years, because they had previously stood as candidates for certain political groups which had subsequently been declared illegal. Although the Government argued that it had derogated from the relevant articles, it provided inadequate information on the existence of any emergency. The HRC found no justification for such a blanket denial of rights. In the absence of necessity, the principle of proportionality indicated a breach of article 25, and Uruguay was under an obligation to enable the applicants once again to participate in political life.[86]

In resolution 46/137, the UN General Assembly reaffirmed that,

> the systematic denial or abridgement of the right to vote on grounds of race or colour is a gross violation of human rights and an affront to the conscience and dignity of mankind, and...the right to participate in a political system based on common and equal citizenship and universal franchise is essential for the exercise of the principle of periodic and genuine elections.

---

85   Countries denying the vote to military personnel include Brazil (below the rank of sergeant), Colombia, Dominican Republic, Ecuador, Guatemala, Honduras, Paraguay, Peru, Uruguay (below the rank of corporal), Venezuela, Chad, Kuwait, Senegal and Tunisia. Indonesia is a special case, for although military personnel are barred from voting, 100 of the 500 seats in the House of Representatives are reserved for retired or active members of the armed forces, appointed by the President of the Republic.

86   Human Rights Committee, Annual Report 1981: UN doc. A/36/40, p. 153. See also *Massera v Uruguay*: Human Rights Committee, Annual Report 1979: UN doc. A/34/40, p. 124, cited in Sieghart, *Human Rights*, 365. In Application 6573/74: 1 *Decisions and Reports* 87, the European Commission of Human Rights upheld a Dutch law depriving persons convicted of 'uncitizenlike' behaviour during the Second World War of their right to vote for life. Cited in Sieghart, *Human Rights*, 363.

The principle of non-discrimination today goes beyond race, to include religion, sex, social group, political opinion or other irrelevant consideration. An electoral system which denied the vote to minority populations, or which disenfranchised half the citizenry, for example, by excluding women,[87] would be incompatible with international standards, and incapable of reflecting the 'will of the people'.

In a society of nation States that defines its members, inter alia, by reference to a population presumed subject to the territorial sovereign, the basic criterion for participation in national political life is clearly citizenship. The international legal principles of non-discrimination and proportionality[88] significantly limit the freedom of States to condition the right to vote, as is evidenced by the small range of permissible restrictions illustrated above. From recognition of the individual right to vote flows the necessity of voter registration machinery, without which, in the majority of cases, there can be no effective exercise of that right.

3.1.5 Voter registration

Giving practical effect to the right of those eligible to vote raises more serious problems. Formally recognizing the right to vote is only part of the issue, for substantial opportunities exist to frustrate the exercise of that right, for example, by obstructing access to the necessary documentation, or otherwise interfering with or discouraging registration. In El Salvador, for example, voter registration was all the more difficult because of the destruction of registries during the civil war, with resulting loss of records. Coupled with significant internal displacement, this made the task of obtaining substitute documentation even harder.

The 'electoral list' is thus a crucial feature in the organization of free and fair elections. Such a system, suggests a recent commentator, must be designed to enable all qualified citizens to be included, to prevent electoral abuse and fraud by individuals, special interest groups, political parties and governments; and be 'widely accepted as an authoritative and legitimate

---

87   Only male citizens over 21 are entitled to vote in Kuwait: IPU, *Chronicle of Parliamentary Elections and Developments*, No. 24, 1989-1990, 109. In Egypt, male electors are registered automatically and women on request; voting is compulsory only for men: ibid., No. 25, 1990-1991, 65-6.

88   Considered in the sense described above in note 6.

means of cataloguing the electoral population and of settling disputes'.[89]
As the Commonwealth Observer Group to the 1992 presidential elections
in Ghana put it:[90]

> An electoral roll of acceptable completeness and accuracy lies at the heart
> of the democratic process where the ability to vote depends on whether a
> voter's name is on the roll. It is also the centre-piece of any meaningful
> door-to-door campaigning and is fundamental to the discharge by party
> polling agents of their duties on polling day.

Accuracy is important, especially so in proportional representation systems
that employ multi-member constituencies, but how to ensure a credible
registration system is no simple matter. Few countries will be able, like
Denmark, to update their voting registers continuously and automatically,
as information is supplied by local authorities.[91] On occasion,
'self-registration' may be enough,[92] but positive governmental action will
often be essential in situations of transition. In the United Kingdom, annual
registers are compiled through forms sent to every household requiring all
those living there and eligible to vote to be listed; house visits are also
undertaken (and in Canada visits by 'enumerators' are the rule). Provisional
lists are drawn up and published, subject to objections; these are decided
by the electoral registration officer, from whom appeal lies to the county
court. The final list is then deposited in public libraries and some other
public buildings.[93] Experience shows that involving political parties and
special interest groups in promoting, monitoring and auditing the
registration process is often called for, together with extensive civic
education programmes, including training election officials, and getting the

---

89   Courtney, John C., 'Introduction,' in Courtney, John C., ed., *Registering Voters:
Comparative Perspectives,* The Center for International Affairs. Harvard University, (1991), at 1-2. The
first multi-party elections in the Comoros in Nov. 1992, for example, were marred by the government's
refusal to update voting lists: Inter-Parliamentary Union, *Chronicle of Parliamentary Elections and
Developments,* No. 27, 1992-1993, 63-5.
90   Commonwealth Observer Group, *Ghana 1992,* 17.
91   ECPRD, *Electoral System Legislation,* 53-4.
92   Whether self-registration promotes voter turn-out is another matter; see Wolfinger,
Raymond E., 'The Politics of Voter Registration Reform,' in Courtney, John C., ed., *Registering Voters:
Comparative Perspectives,* The Center for International Affairs. Harvard University, (1991), 28.
93   Ibid., 471.

voting message across to the public,[94] for example, on how and where to register, and the rights and responsibilities of living in a democracy.[95]

At a practical level, the process of voter registration requires clear eligibility criteria[96] and their consistent application by trained officials. Depending on the method used, whether voluntary registration or official enumeration, those eligible should be aware of the procedure. Electoral lists should be published promptly, and clear effective means should be available for correcting errors, including omissions and cancellation of those deceased or who have moved.[97] The Joint International Observer Group which covered the Malawi national referendum in June 1993 found that voters generally were aware of what to do, as a result of radio announcements and campaign activities by special interest groups, churches, and at public events. The Malawi Referendum Commission also had the specific duty to *promote* registration and civic education, and inconsistent application of policy was most usually due to lack of training.[98]

Many recent elections have been criticised precisely because deficiencies in voter registration, other than minor omissions, have cast

94   The June 1990 elections in Czechoslovakia were preceded by a concerted 'get out the vote campaign'; as one Prague poster put it, 'Everyone who doesn't vote, votes for totalitarianism.' Approximately 95% of eligible voters participated: US Commission, *Central and Eastern Europe 1990*, 126, 132.

95   Jeffrey Fischer, 'Voter Registration in Emerging Democracies. Two Case Studies: Haiti 1990; Guyana 1991,' in Courtney, John C., ed. *Registering Voters: Comparative Perspectives*. The Center for International Affairs. Harvard University, (1991), 55.

96   See Brick, Gastil & Kimberling, *Mongolia 1992*, 18, noting that it was unclear how voter lists were prepared, and recommending a nation-wide computerized civil registry from which the Central Election Commission could generate voter lists.

97   See Atwood, Susan J., Villaveces, Marta Maria. *IFES Technical Election Assistance Project, Romania, March 10-September 29. 1992. Report*. International Foundation for Election Systems. Washington, D.C. (1992), 14f, recommending advance publication of the voter registry and that both 'election officials and the political parties must take the responsibility for alerting voters to the need to check these lists'. See also Brunet, Marchand & Neher, *Togo 1992*, 24.

98   JIOG, *Malawi 1993*: 'Rigorous application of the age criteria was unprecedented and at times problematic; local teachers acting as clerks were helpful ... Registration clerks often relied on their personal knowledge of applicants, advice of domestic monitor and testimonials...' (para. 55). Some minor instances of intimidation due to the presence of government party monitors were noted, but otherwise the presence of monitors in the process contributed to a high degree of credibility.

doubt on their fairness.[99] A 1992 report by IFES on the registration system in Ghana cited a variety of technical irregularities with the roll, including an apparently larger-than-statistically-possible number of registered voters, failure to purge those who had died since 1987, double entries resulting from software problems, and inconsistent registration of names.[100] The Commonwealth Observer Group was somewhat more sanguine in its assessment, however, noting that voters' rolls in developing countries tend to have deficiencies of one kind or another. What counts is whether this results from manipulation or muddle, and the potential to affect the outcome of an election;[101] it is not so much the question of errors themselves, as the 'bias' of the list in a particular direction. The Commonwealth Group agreed with IFES that the errors resulted from misinformation rather than a deliberate attempt to affect the results, but criticised IFES's offhand dismissal of the roll and its 'imperative' call for re-registration. Less expensive alternatives had not been considered, and the criticism had merely served to heighten controversy.[102] Even if the number of errors and duplications is high in any particular case, there may be other practical means to prevent double or multiple voting, for example, by marking voters with indelible ink,[103] or by the use of 'tendered votes'.[104] The Group cited experience with the independence vote in Zimbabwe, conducted without a formal voters roll:

99   See National Democratic Institute for International Affairs. 'Executive Summary. February 21, 1993 Presidential Elections in Senegal.' International Delegation Report. Washington, D.C. (1993): errors on electoral lists, electoral cards and national identity cards, coupled with the issue of duplicate electoral cards, tended to disfavour opposition candidates, while the distribution of blank 'ordinances' designed to allow errors of omission to be corrected tended to compromise confidence in the system. National Democratic Institute for International Affairs. 'Preliminary Statement. NDI International Observer Delegation to the Pakistan National Elections,' 8 Oct. 1993: the quality of the electoral rolls was often in doubt, leading to problems in identifying and verifying voters. In both cases, the observer missions did not consider such irregularities sufficient to question the election results overall. See also Commonwealth Observer Group, *Kenya 1992*, 12-14.

100   IFES Report of 1 June 1992, 17, cited in Commonwealth Observer Group, *Ghana 1992*, 11-12.

101   Commonwealth Observer Group, *Ghana 1992*, 12.

102   The Commonwealth Observer Group noted that re-registration would have cost some $14.5 million, to which IFES proposed a US contribution of $200,000: ibid., 14-15; see also the Group's conclusions at 63-5.

103   Ibid., 16. Sometimes the ink turns out to be less than indelible, as happened in Nicaragua in 1990. In the absence of other problems indicating multiple voting, the parties agreed to accept the outcome of the election: Freely Elected Heads, *Nicaragua 1990*, 24.

104   On the use of 'tendered votes' in Cambodia, see IPU, *Report of IPU Election Observer Mission, Cambodia, 16 May-4 June 1993*, 12-13.

...provided the voters' roll is inclusive rather than exclusive (i.e. that it has not been corrupted by the systematic exclusion of particular voters) and provided it affords the electorate at large a reasonable opportunity to vote, it need not be a barrier to a free and fair election provided always that the voters' ink is dependable.

The *security* of the voter registration system is thus as important as its integrity.[105]

Voter registration and the publication of verifiable lists of electors have an important part to play in building and maintaining the confidence of the electorate, and thereby contributing also to ensuring free and fair elections. Given the inherent opportunities for disenfranchising substantial portions of the population through manipulation of the registration process, transparency of process is called for. Political parties have a fundamental role in getting their supporters to register, double-checking provisional lists, and challenging errors. Practice varies between the State responsibility model of registration, through household surveys and visits, and the self-registration model, where the initiative lies with the voter. No rule determines the choice, but circumstances may dictate a pro-active role for the State, for example, in transition situations where both the idea of voting and the possibility of a free choice may be novel experiences. Only if the population at large is aware of the procedures and effectively able to access them, will a resulting election likely be fair.

3.1.6 Civic education and voter information

Civic education and voter information, like other topics mentioned here, might at first seem to fall outside the strict purview of State responsibilities with respect to free and fair elections; in fact, civic education is part of the school curriculum in most established democracies. The Commonwealth Observer Group to the 1991 elections in Zambia considered that 'an intensive and widespread voter education programme about the rights, processes and implications' of the change to a multi-party system was to have been expected. It expressed its disappointment with the apparently

---

105   As one commentator puts it, 'The right to vote...must be accompanied by the right to have one's vote counted without being diluted by votes fraudulently cast.' Kimberling, William C., 'A Rational Approach to Evaluating Alternative Voter Registration Systems and Procedures,', in Courtney, John C., ed. *Registering Voters: Comparative Perspectives.* The Center for International Affairs. Harvard University, (1991), 3.

limited impact of what had been done, and at the failure of the media in particular to contribute to the education of voters.[106] Experience in Ghana in 1992 provided a marked contrast. Posters were widely displayed, with instructions on how to vote, encouraging exercise of the franchise and promoting democratic ideals of tolerance and peaceful political activity. With financial support from foreign government and non-government agencies, education posters, radio and television programmes and booklets were produced and widely distributed, targeting not just voters, but also candidates and political parties;[107] the Commonwealth Observer Group concluded that, 'Across the country, the average voter seemed to be extremely well-informed about the date of the poll, the hours of voting and the procedures to be followed.'[108]

Most observers also agree that UNTAC's education programme in Cambodia was extraordinarily successful, both in terms of resources and effects.[109] As another international delegation report put it recently,[110]

> ...democracy can be defined in very formal terms: fair elections; a free press; and multiple parties. However, to establish a pluralist system requires more...An environment must exist in which the values of democracy are understood and acted upon by the population...Such an environment is not something that simply emerges. It is a consequence of actions by people in leadership positions. The government can play an important role in stimulating activity...through non-partisan civic education programs that promote democratic values among the adult population and that form an essential part of the general education curriculum. Political parties, civic organizations and the media have an important role to play in this connection.

Again, the principle of effectiveness of obligations, supported by the actual practice of States in situations marked by deficiencies in this field,[111] such

106 Commonwealth Secretariat, *Presidential and National Assembly Elections in Zambia, 31 October 1991*, Report of the Commonwealth Observer Group, (1992), 12 (hereafter Commonwealth Observer Group, *Zambia 1991*).

107 Commonwealth Observer Group, *Ghana 1992*, 26-8; Annexes VII-IX.

108 Ibid., 65.

109 See generally, IPU, *Report of IPU Election Observer Mission, Cambodia, 16 May-4 June 1993*.

110 NDI, *Senegal 1991*, 38.

111 Brunet, Marchand & Neher, *Togo 1992*, at 1, recommending a vigorous programme of civic education particularly since most Togolese had never experienced either free elections or democracy.

as lack of experience with voting in a democratic environment with 'real' choices, shows how both civic education and voter information can be central in attaining the objective of a free and fair election. Election observation missions have repeatedly stressed the necessity for civic education, voter information and poll worker training,[112] confirming the necessity for active programmes in situations of transition or change if the result is to be truly representative of the will of the people. As with voter registration, a passive government policy, leaving education to political parties, churches and NGOs, may not be sufficient to establish the basic conditions for the conduct of a free and fair election.

3.1.7 Candidates, political parties and political organization

By contrast with some of the other indices of free and fair elections, candidates, political parties and political organization fall more easily within traditional notions of human rights. Article 25 of the Covenant on Civil and Political Rights, for example, provides that every citizen has the right, without discrimination, to take part in the conduct of public affairs, to be elected, and to have equal access to public service in his or her country. Those rights are not absolute, however, and may be subject to a variety of reasonable limitations. A State's choice of electoral system, for example, may directly affect the freedom of individuals to present themselves as candidates for election, otherwise than through a recognized political party. 'Threshold' requirements can also limit the representation possibilities for parties that fail to obtain a certain percentage of the vote.[113] Registration criteria may effectively prevent the formation of political parties, while State monopolies over certain resources, such as funding, meeting places, transport, printing presses and the media may hinder even minimal political organization. Some of the limitations on individual candidatures are mentioned above, and other restrictions are dealt with below in the context of electoral campaigns. The CSCE standard, for example, emphasizes the

---

112   In addition to the examples cited above, see National Democratic Institute for International Affairs. 'Executive Summary. February 21, 1993 Presidential Elections in Senegal.' International Delegation Report. Washington, D.C. 1993; National Democratic Institute for International Affairs. Council of Freely Elected Heads of Government. 'Preliminary Post-Election Statement. International Delegation to the National Elections in Paraguay.' 10 May 1993. Asunción, Paraguay. Note also the work of civic organizations and the Central Election Commission in Bulgaria: NDI/NRI, *Bulgaria 1990*, 26-7, 31-2.

113   See above, section 3.1.1. The 5% threshold in the December 1993 Russian election appears to have been intended especially to keep out small, 'troublesome' parties: US Commission, *Russia 1993*, 4.

necessity for *choice*, by requiring a clear separation between State and political parties, and in particular that political parties not be merged with the State.[114]

Within the European context, article 3 of the First Protocol has come to be interpreted as guaranteeing freedom of choice, which in turn implies freedom to present oneself for election, as well as freedom of political organization.[115] The European Commission on Human Rights has held that the banning of political parties violated article 3. Parties must have reasonable opportunities to present their candidates for election, but may nonetheless be subject to certain conditions affecting, for example, registration and funding.[116] Looking at the 'general conditions' of the electoral process, the Inter-American Commission on Human Rights has deduced the requirement that the different political groups must be allowed to participate under equal circumstances; they should 'all have similar basic conditions for conducting their campaign'.[117] It criticised the Sandinistas in its 1983-84 Annual Report for having used all the resources of the State to put itself at an advantage.[118] Similar criticism was levelled at Chile with respect to the 1978 referendum and the 1980 plebiscite.[119]

Commonwealth observer groups have also repeatedly called for 'de-linking the ruling party from the government.' As one Group put it,[120]

Recent Commonwealth experience suggests that at the political level two elements are of particular importance to the conduct of free and fair elections during the transition from a one-party to a multi-party system:

114   CSCE: Declaration of the Copenhagen Meeting: 29 I.L.M. 1305 (1990), para. (5.4). Lack of choice generally will be sufficient to prejudice the outcome of an election; a French parliamentary delegation to a recent presidential election in an African State, boycotted by the two principal opposition candidates, concluded that the elections 'n'avaient pas eu lieu dans des conditions satisfaisantes en raison du caractère non contradictoire de ce scrutin, et que leur déroulement posait plus de questions qu'il n'apportait de réponses'. *Bulletin de l'Assemblée Nationale*, no. 14 du 5 oct. 1993, 61-2.

115   Goy, 'La garantie européenne du droit à de libres élections législatives,' 1301-2.

116   A provision requiring would-be registered parties to obtain a certain number of signatures (between one and five hundred) as a pre-condition to acceptance was upheld as reasonable: Goy, 'La garantie européenne du droit à de libres élections législatives,' 1302, although in the December 1993 Russian elections fairly onerous signature requirements (100,000) were identified as a source of problems: US Commission, *Russia 1993*, 8, 15.

117   *Final Report on Cases 9768, 9780 and 9828:* IACmHR, 97, para. 49: OEA/Ser.L/V/II.77, doc. 7, rev. 1 (1990); text in Buergenthal, T. and Norris, R.E., *Human Rights: The Inter-American System*, Part 3, Cases and Decisions, Booklet 21.6, Release 93-1, p. 77, 89.

118   Ibid., para. 52.

119   Ibid., para. 54, citing its earlier reports.

120   Commonwealth Observer Group, *Kenya 1992*, 7.

the creation of a 'level playing field' for the lawful activities of all political parties and a thorough de-linking of government affairs, personnel and resources from those of the ruling party.

In practice, such identification has proven difficult to unravel at the moment of transition, for example, in the 1992 elections in Kenya[121] and Ghana,[122] the 1991 Zambia elections,[123] or in the July 1992 Nigerian parliamentary elections. On the latter occasion, only two political parties were allowed to participate; both were created by the (military) administration, which also funded their organization and activities, and wrote their manifestos.[124] Once again, principles of reasonableness and proportionality show at which point such restrictions render elections unfair.

Article 25 of the 1966 Covenant on Civil and Political Rights confirms the entitlement of every citizen to take part in the conduct of public affairs, to vote and to be elected. State practice in turn confirms that this right is not absolute, but may be subject to reasonable limitations, and the *criteria for individual candidature* commonly follow those necessary for voting: minimum age, residence and absence of disqualification.[125] The rationale for certain conditions such as age or residence is obvious: a sufficient level

---

121   Ibid., vii: 'The process of decoupling ... was not undertaken with the degree of commitment necessary ... and ... the time within which that decoupling could have taken place was too short.'; see also at ix, 39

122   Commonwealth Observer Group, *Ghana 1992*, 63.

123   Commonwealth Observer Group, *Zambia 1991*, 9-10; NDI/Carter Center, *Zambia 1991*, 43-4. See also Commonwealth Secretariat, *Referendum on the Draft Constitution in Seychelles, 12-15 November 1992*, Report of the Commonwealth Observer Group, (1992), 12 (hereafter Commonwealth Observer Group, *Seychelles November 1992*); with respect to the Democratic People's Republic of Korea, see Inter-Parliamentary Union, *Chronicle of Parliamentary Elections and Developments*, No. 24, 1989-1990, 61-2; and for Cuba, see *Keesing's Record of World Events*, News Digest for February 1993.

124   Inter-Parliamentary Union, *Chronicle of Parliamentary Elections and Developments*, No. 27, 1992-1993, 169-71. Following the election, with a significantly low turnout, the new legislature was not allowed to start sitting after all, as the military regime argued that it would be unconstitutional before an elected President was sworn in. Presidential elections were duly held in June 1993, and subsequently annulled by the military.

125   For a summary account of qualifications, see IPU, *Electoral Systems: A World-Wide Comparative Survey*, Geneva, (1993). The Romanian electoral law prohibited the participation of those 'who have committed abuses in political, judicial and administrative functions, who have infringed upon fundamental human rights, as well as those people who have organized or who have been instruments of repression in the service of the security forces, the former police and militia forces.' Carothers, T., 'Romania,' in Garber & Bjornlund, *New Democratic Frontier*, at 81, finds no evidence that it was ever applied.

of maturity and connection to the community.[126] Other limitations in turn may seek to protect the integrity of the system, for example, by excluding those whose independence may be threatened by legislative responsibilities, such as judges and civil servants; or who may be tempted by the possibility for material benefits, such as public contractors.[127] European jurisprudence recognizes a variety of conditions and exclusions, including penal detention and residence requirements, but provides generally that they shall be prescribed by law and reasonably necessary in a democratic society. They must also not be arbitrary or violate the principle of non-discrimination.[128] The Inter-American Commission on Human Rights has interpreted the entitlement of the State to develop its internal life freely as nevertheless subject to the obligation to respect the rights of individuals, specifically as recognized in the American Convention on Human Rights.[129]

Substantive or ideological obstacles to participation, however, may well violate the individual right to participate in public affairs, particularly given the provisions of article 19 of the Covenant and the principle of non-discrimination. Candidates in Indonesia must be loyal to *Pancasila* as the basic ideology of the State; in Iran, unless of a recognized religious minority, they must have a belief in and active obligation to Islam and the prevailing system of government; in Portugal, they are disqualified if they held important public positions before 1 April 1974, and did not clearly repudiate the regime then in power before that date; in Iraq, they must uphold the principles and aims of the July 1968 revolution.[130] The prevailing jurisprudence on denial or restriction of political rights indicates that such measures will violate individual rights if unreasonable, arbitrary or disproportionate; while the State may be free, for example, to restrict the activities of those who previously abused a position of executive or legislative authority, to deny political rights merely on the basis of political opinion poses a direct challenge to the democratic process itself.

126　The European Commission on Human Rights upheld age limits of 25 (House of Representatives) and 40 (Senate) in Belgium: Application 6745-6/74 (*W,X,Y & Z v. Belgium*): 2 *Decisions and Reports* 110; cited in Sieghart, *Human Rights*, 363-4.

127　The latter are expressly barred from being candidates for election in Costa Rica: Inter-Parliamentary Union, *Chronicle of Parliamentary Elections and Developments*, No. 24, 1989-1990, 53.

128　Goy, 'La garantie européenne du droit à de libres élections législatives,' 1316-24.

129　*Final Report on Cases 9768, 9780 and 9828:* IACmHR, 97, paras. 94, 99-102. Above, note 117.

130　See Inter-Parliamentary Union, *Chronicle of Parliamentary Elections and Developments*, No. 26, 1991-1992, 79, 83, 133; ibid., No. 23, 1988-1989, 49.

Other, technical requirements can also constitute obstacles to effective political participation. Entitlement to stand as a candidate, for example, often requires nomination by a political party,[131] although independent candidates may sometimes qualify in their own right.[132]

Registration requirements for political parties can operate both as formal and as substantive restrictions. The governing criterion will be how those requirements work in practice. Although the 1991 Senegalese electoral code contained no restrictions on parties, some opposition groups argued that the requirement for payment of a deposit for ballot printing, reimbursable only if the party obtained a certain percentage of the vote, was unfair to smaller parties with limited funding.[133] Though such a 'threshold' might serve the legitimate purpose of restricting truly marginal parties, the NDI assessment recommended that alternative methods be considered. Togo's 1991 law, the Political Parties' Charter, describes the duties of political parties, the regulations governing their creation, finances and penalties for contravention. A minimum of 30 persons is required to set up a political party, coming from two thirds of the prefectures in the country. Application is made to the Ministry of the Interior and, if everything is in order, the party must thereafter publish basic information about the organization in the official gazette and another journal. Approved parties may present candidates at elections.[134] In Mexico, a political party may be registered if it has at least 3,000 members in each one of at least half the States of Mexico or at least 300 members in each of at least half the single-member constituencies; in either case, the total number of members

131   Cf. the Dominican Republic, in which candidates must be nominated by a political party recognized by the Central Electoral Board; independent candidates may only stand if they are backed by a political group that has an organization and a programme similar to that of a political party: Inter-Parliamentary Union, *Chronicle of Parliamentary Elections and Developments*, No. 24, 1989-1990, 67.

132   In Bulgaria, for example, this required obtaining the signatures of 500 citizens: NDI/NRI, *Bulgaria 1990*, 30. Electoral law revisions in the Baltic States and the Soviet Republics in 1989 opened the way to broader-based candidacies. The 1989 Latvian Law on Elections to the Supreme Soviet laid down a minimum age of 21 for candidates, who must also have lived in Latvia for ten years. Previously, only the Communist Party, labour collectives and other public organizations had been permitted to nominate candidates; the new law extended to any public or political organization having at least one hundred members. See also US Commission on Security and Cooperation in Europe, *Elections in the Baltic States and Soviet Republics*, Washington, D.C., (1990), 62f, 100f, 126.

133   Financial deposits are a common requirement also for individual candidates, with forfeiture or reimbursement determined by the numbers of votes polled; in the United Kingdom, candidates lose their £500 deposit if they fail to poll at least 5% of the vote.

134   Brunet, Marchand & Neher, *Togo 1992*, 20. IFES recommended extending certain administrative deadlines and, in order to protect the process from political influence, that accreditation of political parties should be entrusted to an electoral commission.

must be not less than 65,000.[135] The *Comprehensive Settlement Agreement* for Cambodia provided that political parties could be formed by any group of five thousand registered voters, but also required that party platforms be consistent with the principles and objectives of the Agreement. Party affiliation was required to stand for election to the constituent assembly, and UNTAC was made responsible for determining whether parties and candidates qualified for participation in the election.[136]

From time to time governments ban particular political parties. The European Commission on Human Rights has ruled that the benefit of Protocol 1, article 3 of the European Convention cannot be claimed by those who would participate in elections for a purpose incompatible with article 17, namely, to destroy the very rights and freedoms protected.[137] Relying on the *travaux préparatoires*, the European Commission also rejected the complaint of the applicant in *German Communist Party v. Federal Republic of Germany* that it had been dissolved and its property confiscated contrary to articles 9, 10 and 11 of the Convention. The European Commission noted that the avowed aim of the party was to establish a communist society by means of a proletarian revolution and the 'dictatorship of the proletariat'; this would entail the suppression of various rights and freedoms protected by the Convention.[138] During the 1990 elections, the Electoral Commission in the former German Democratic Republic banned the neo-nazi West German Republikaner Party or any local branch from running candidates,

---

135   Inter-Parliamentary Union, *Chronicle of Parliamentary Elections and Developments*, No. 26, 1991-1992, 113. Parties applying for registration in Ghana were required to list members in all regions of the country and to have offices in at least two-thirds of the districts in each region. Members of the party leadership were to be resident in separate districts, 'in order to ensure a truly national character': Commonwealth Observer Group, *Ghana 1992*, 6.

136   *Comprehensive Settlement Agreement for Cambodia*, Elections Annex (Annex 3), arts. 5-7:31 I.L.M. 180 (1992). Cf. David Hearst and Jonathan Steele, 'Russian parties barred from poll,' *The Guardian Weekly*, 21 Nov. 1993, p. 7: Russia's Electoral Commission barred eight political groupings — a third of the field — from putting up candidates in the elections for the new parliament, scheduled for 12 December 1993. It was claimed that the eight blocs had failed to achieve either the 100,000 signature threshold required under the law, or the requirement not to get more than 15 per cent of signatures from only one region. The Russian All People's Union claimed, however, that the police had confiscated 22,000 signatures on the day before the registration deadline. See also US Commission, *Russia 1993*, 8-9, 16.

137   *Glimmerveen and Hagenbeek v. Netherlands* (Applications 8348/78 and 8406/78): 18 *Decisions and Reports* 187; cited in Sieghart, *Human Rights*, 363. Art. 17 provides: 'Nothing in this Convention may be interpreted as implying for any State, group or person any right to engage in any activity or perform any act aimed at the destruction of any of the rights and freedoms set forth herein or at their limitation to a greater extent than is provided for in the Convention.'

138   Application 250/57: 1 *Yearbook* 222; cited in Sieghart, *Human Rights*, 105-6; see also Fawcett, J.E.S., *The Application of the European Convention on Human Rights*, (2nd ed., 1987), 314-6.

relying on the electoral law prohibition on parties or political associations that express hatred against denominations, races and peoples, or which engage in war propaganda. The ban provoked no controversy.

Bulgarian legislation permitted the banning of parties based on religious or ethnic principles, although none was so proscribed during the 1990 elections.[139] Ghanaian regulations prohibited the use of signs, symbols or slogans which identified groups with any particular region, ethnic origin, religion or profession.[140] The registration of the Islamic Party of Kenya was rejected in 1992, on the ground that it was 'a religious group subject to foreign interests and ... because it was deemed to be a threat to national security.'[141]

Funding for political parties can raise difficult issues, particularly in situations of transition, for example, where the ruling party maintains a significant monopoly on public resources, or where external influence is feared.[142] In Nicaragua for the 1990 elections, the Supreme Electoral Council was authorized to allocate a specific amount to political parties, fifty per cent of which was to be divided between them in equal amounts, and the remainder on the basis of the numbers of votes received in the 1984 elections. Parties which did not contest the earlier ballot each received the same as the party with the fewest votes. Funds could also be received from abroad, half the amount going to the party in question, and the other half to the Supreme Electoral Council.[143] There was no bar on receiving overseas funds for the 1990 Czechoslovakia elections; otherwise, public funding turned on the percentage of votes received. Parties failing to receive 2 per cent received nothing, and those with more than 2 per cent received 10 crowns for each vote.[144] The Hungarian Parliament allocated a total of 700

139   NDI/NRI, *Bulgaria 1990*, 20, 23-4.

140   Commonwealth Observer Group, *Ghana 1992*, 6-7,

141   Commonwealth Observer Group, *Kenya 1992*, 6. The Green Party and the Green Party of Kenya were also denied registration for 'security reasons.'

142   Operative para. 6 of UNGA res. 46/130, 'Respect for the principles of national sovereignty and non-interference in the internal affairs of States in their electoral processes,' adopted 17 Dec. 1991 by 102 votes in favour, 40 against and 13 abstentions, '*Strongly appeals* to all States to refrain from financing or providing, directly or indirectly, any other form of overt or covert support for political parties or groups and from taking actions to undermine the electoral processes in any country...' This is repeated in UNGA resolutions 47/130, 18 Dec. 1992 and 48/124, 20 Dec. 1993.

143   Organization of American States Secretary General. *Observation of the Electoral Process, Nicaragua 1989-90*. Observers' Guide. 1989.

144   US Commission, *Central and Eastern Europe*, 127. Not surprisingly, considerable financial and material support was extended by West German to East German parties in the 1990 elections: ibid., 15-16.

million forints (US$11.2 million) for opposition parties in 1990, which received grants initially on the basis of unverified membership claims.[145] Private fund-raising from inside and outside the country was also permitted, save that contributions from foreign governments were prohibited.[146] State subsidies for political parties were also payable in Romania, to cover initial costs and thereafter on the basis of the number of candidates fielded. Parties complained of late receipt of funds, putting them at a substantial disadvantage where the ruling party retained control of public resources.[147]

How much political parties are able to spend can clearly have an impact on the outcome of an election. Both a French parliamentary delegation to the Seychelles in July 1993 and the Commonwealth Observer Group in November registered a number of complaints, including the lack of balance in the resources of the parties.[148] How such balance can or should be maintained does not permit of any ready answer; the Commonwealth Observer Group in November 1992 considered that the details were a 'local political matter for the Government and the parties to resolve,' even though it also recognized the necessity to fund parties during the transition period.[149] Moreover, the US Supreme Court has held that expenditure limitations are unconstitutional, since they place substantial direct restrictions on political expression and as such are prohibited by the First Amendment.[150]

The established democracies have come up with mixed responses to the issue of government funding, private contributions, and campaign expenses. In France, public financing is limited to 10% of the maximum 500,000 francs allowed per candidate, and private contributions are

145   Ibid., 38. Also, Melia, T.O., 'Hungary,' in Garber & Bjornlund, *New Democratic Frontier*, 39, 53-4. The smaller parties objected to this system of apportionment, but it was maintained; although required to account for their funding, few parties had done so by the end of 1990.

146   US Commission, *Central and Eastern Europe*, 38.

147   US Commission, *Central and Eastern Europe*, 111; see also with respect to Slovenia (p.64) and Croatia (p.85).

148   *Bulletin de l'Assemblée Nationale*, no. 14 du 5 oct.1993, 61; Commonwealth Observer Group, *Seychelles November 1992*, 14. The July mission was present for the election of a Constitutional Commission, which was also monitored by the Commonwealth; the November mission monitored the referendum on the draft Constitution.

149   Commonwealth Observer Group, *Seychelles November 1992*, 14.

150   Limitations may be valid, however, where candidates adhere to them in order to receive public funding: Inter-Parliamentary Union, *Chronicle of Parliamentary Elections and Developments*, No. 25, 1990-1991, 125.

regulated.[151] In the United Kingdom, the expenses of individual candidates are limited at general elections, but no restrictions apply to national advertising campaigns by political parties. Candidates must appoint an election agent to pay and account for their expenses, and to submit returns within thirty-five days of the election.[152]

Money played an important role in the December 1993 Russian elections. Limited financing for parties/blocs and individuals was available from the Central and District Election Commissions, contributions from foreign governments and entities were forbidden, but otherwise there were no controls and substantial sums were spent, for example, by Zhironovsky, to purchase expensive television time.[153] As Jean Gicquel has remarked, 'Les principales causes d'inégalités contre lesquelles il s'agit de se prémunir, au tant de moins de lutter, sont l'argent et les faveurs de pouvoir.[154]'

The rationale for public funding of political parties and election expenses is usually linked to the desirability of establishing, as far as possible, a 'level playing field'. Other reasons identified by Jean-Claude Masclet include a combination of freedom of association with the sovereignty of the people public funding makes the political right *effective*.[155] It may also incidentally help to keep political parties independent of financial pressure, in situations where the role of parties is complex and often controversial.[156]

Democracy in practice, which requires choice between alternatives, needs at least two competing political parties, although competition that is too divisive defeats its purpose. In situations of transition, political parties

151   ECPRD, *Electoral System Legislation*, 261. For a more detailed account, see Masclet, Jean-Claude, *Droit électoral*, (1989), 244-65. Public funding lined to previous electoral performance has been upheld by the European Commission of Human Rights; see Application 6850/74: 5 *Decisions and Reports* 90.

152   See Representation of the People Act 1983, sections 72-90; breaches attract severe penalties. In 1993, the limits (which may vary slightly depending on the type of election and type of constituency) were, for a county constituency in a general election, £4,330 plus 4.9p for every entry in the register of electors. See ECPRD, *Electoral System Legislation*, 469, 477.

153   US Commission, *Russia 1993*, 27.

154   Gicquel, J., *Droit constitutionnel et institutions politiques.* 12ème ed., 1993, 139.

155   'En d'autre termes, il existe pour l'Etat non seulement une faculté de financement public pour rendre la liberté et l'égalité effectives, mais aussi une obligation dans certaines circonstances qu'il appartient au législateur d'apprécier': Masclet, Jean-Claude, *Droit électoral*, (1989), 251.

156   For a summary account of some of the issues, see Pinto-Duschinsky, M., 'The Role of Political Parties,' in International Foundation for Election Systems. *Central European Electoral Systems Symposium, Budapest, July 30-August 2, 1991*. International Foundation for Election Systems. Washington, D.C., (1991), 74.

often face difficulties in establishing themselves, or in engaging in meaningful campaigns in face of monopolies of power and resources. Neither public nor external aid can be ruled out as impermissible, provided that generally they contribute to healthy debate within a strengthening democratic process. Where they become substitutes for grass roots support and effective local organization, however, then they may also cease to contribute to channelling the will of the people into genuine elections. Clearly, a free and fair election is less likely if the government denies financial resources to its opponents, while using all the resources at its disposal to put the opposition at a disadvantage. Equally, in theory at least, unlimited expenditure by any party can result in a distorted electoral process. The art is to find that balance which best accommodates the objective of allowing each party a reasonable opportunity to put across its message; this may well entail a combination of public funding with election expenditure controls.

3.1.8 Electoral campaigns

Systems and legal guarantees are only a part of the equation that produces a free and fair election. How procedures are actually applied and what happens in practice will ultimately determine whether the people have been able freely to express their will. Commenting on the inter-American system, the Inter-American Commission on Human Rights has remarked on the 'direct relationship' between political rights and 'representative democracy as a form of the organization of the State, which at the same time presupposes the observance of other basic human rights':[157]

representatives...are elected by the citizens to apply certain political measures, which...implies the prior existence of an ample political debate on the nature of the policies to be applied freedom of expression between organized political groups freedom of association that have had the opportunity to express themselves and meet publicly freedom of assembly.

The rule of law, moreover, above the will of the leaders, is essential to 'preserve the purity of the expression of the popular will'.[158]

---

157 *Final Report on Cases 9768, 9780 and 9828:* IACmHR, 97, para. 41. Above note 185.
158 Ibid., para. 42.

A successful election does not depend solely on what happens on ballot day; the totality of the process must be examined, including preliminary issues such as the nature of the electoral system, voter entitlement, voter registration, party organization and civic education.[159] The indices of a free and fair election are especially important with respect to the conduct of the election campaign, at which point a number of fundamental human rights come into play, together with the responsibility of the State, as described in article 2 of the 1966 Covenant on Civil and Political Rights,

> to respect and to ensure to all individuals within its territory and subject to its jurisdiction the rights recognized in the present Covenant, without distinction of any kind, such as race, colour, sex, language, religion, political or other opinion, national or social origin, property, birth or other status.

Specifically, national and international observers will need to know whether freedom of movement, assembly, association and expression have been respected throughout the election period; whether all parties have conducted their political activities within the law; whether any political party or special interest group has been subjected to arbitrary and unnecessary restrictions in regard to access to the media or generally in regard to their freedom to communicate their views; whether parties, candidates and supporters have enjoyed equal security; whether voters have been able to cast their ballots freely, without fear or intimidation; whether the secrecy of the ballot has been maintained; and whether the overall conduct of the ballot has been such as to avoid fraud and illegality.[160]

The essentially human rights dimension to many political and electoral rights should not be ignored, so far as some of those applicable in the elections context may not be subject to any derogation whatsoever, while others may only be restricted in accordance with law and, among other

---

159   For an overview of basic issues, see IPU, Questionnaire concerning Parliamentary Elections: IPU doc. CHR/93/1; OAS Secretary General, Observation of the Electoral Process, Nicaragua, 1989-90, Observers' Guide; Council of Europe, *Handbook for Observers of Elections*, Strasbourg, 1992.

160   Cf. Council of Europe, *Handbook for Observers of Elections*, Strasbourg, 1992; Organization of American States Secretary-General, *Observation of the Electoral Process, Nicaragua 1989-90, Observers' Guide*, n.d. See also the various 'checklists' and 'observation notes' annexed to Commonwealth Observer Group reports; for example, *Malaysia 1990; Bangladesh 1991; Zambia 1991; Kenya 1992; Ghana 1992.*

limitations, to the extent reasonably necessary in a democratic society.[161] The settled jurisprudence of the United Nations Human Rights Committee and of regional protection mechanisms in Europe and the Americas confirms not only that the permissible areas of derogation must be interpreted restrictively, but also that the very derogations themselves can be subject to review.[162]

Notwithstanding the elements of appreciation involved, the effect of deficiencies or weaknesses in one or more fields must be weighed against the international free and fair elections standard. Perhaps not surprisingly, few elections in situations of transition allow for clear *fair/not fair* assessments; indeed, the role of observer missions is often not so much to engage in an isolated verification exercise, as to facilitate the growth of democracy and the building of strong national institutions.[163] Typical instructions to Commonwealth observer groups, for example, emphasize the origins of their mission in a government invitation, supported by the political parties. The task of such a group is to observe every relevant aspect of the organization and conduct of the election in accordance with the law of the country concerned. It is to determine, in its impartial judgment and in the context of that law, whether the election or vote has been free and fair. However, it has no executive role, and is neither to supervise nor to act as a commission of inquiry.[164]

Just as democracy is not founded on a single ballot, so an election does not become *un*free or *un*fair solely by reason of one or more breaches of

161   The circumstances that may justify restrictions tend to vary with the right concerned; see the 1966 Covenant on Civil and Political Rights, for example, in particular art. 12(3)—freedom of movement; art. 19(3)—freedom of expression; art. 21—freedom of assembly; art. 22(2)—freedom of association.

162   See for example on the interpretation and application of art. 9(3): McGoldrick, D., *The Human Rights Committee,* (1991), 461-71; and on restrictions and limitations generally, Sieghart, P., *The International Law of Human Rights,* (1983), 85-103.

163   See Pierre Cornillon, Secretary General, Inter-Parliamentary Union, 'Rights and Responsibilities of Election Observers,' IPU, Geneva, Mar. 1994.

164   The Observer Group reports to the Commonwealth Secretary General and to the Government of the country concerned, and thereafter to the leadership of the political parties contesting the vote. The terms of reference for such observer missions are more or less identical; see, for example, those for the mission to observe the constitutional referendum in Seychelles in November 1992: Commonwealth Observer Group, *Seychelles November 1992,* 2. Adopted in Zimbabwe in 1991, the Harare Commonwealth Declaration established as a priority the promotion of the association's fundamental political values, including democracy, democratic processes and institutions which reflect national circumstances, human rights, the rule of law, and just and honest government. Heads of Government agreed that, besides advice and technical assistance, one way to strengthen democracy was to assist members to reinforce their election and other constitutional processes through the institution of observer missions at the request of member governments: Commonwealth Observer Group, *Ghana 1992,* 1-2.

international standards. In many cases, too, the observer's task will be to help establish the range of permissible variation from the standard norm, applying the relevant international standards to particular local circumstances. Here, it will often be necessary to ask whether the 'wrong' done in fact had an impact on the election; this reflects international law's concern with *results*, rather than with 'technical' infringements. In this context of progressive development, the observer's responsibility is certainly to pinpoint egregious violations of election rights, but also to keep them in context and to indicate how and where improvements can be made.[165]

On occasion, however, either the basic conditions or the cumulative effect of incidents may tip the balance to a negative assessment. In November 1993, for example, the US Department of State was reported as saying that elections in Equatorial Guinea risked becoming a parody of democracy, because of the brutality and repression of the regime.[166] Different perspectives may nevertheless produce different assessments. The December 1992 Kenya Elections were also judged by some observers not to have met the free and fair standard. The Attorney General attempted to shorten the nomination process for opposition parties; legislation preventing meetings of more than three persons without a permit was used to prevent opposition rallies; journalists and opposition activists were arrested and detained without charge; and villages were attacked, crops burnt and meetings disrupted throughout the campaign.[167] The Commonwealth Observer Group's final assessment was that the elections constituted an important turning point:[168]

165   See for example the general conclusions of French parliamentary delegations to observe elections in Pakistan, Seychelles, Central African Republic, Burundi, Djibouti and Senegal during the course of 1993: *Bulletin de l'Assemblée Nationale*, no. 7 du 8 juin 1993, 43, 44; no. 8 du 15 juin 1993, 43; no. 14 du 5 oct. 1993, 61, 62; no. 16 du 20 oct. 1993, 44-5. Cf. *Keesing's Record of World Events, News Digest for March 1993*, 39251, reporting Lesotho's general election in the presence of some 130 observers from 29 countries under the auspices of the UN as 'free and fair', despite some shortcomings in the distribution of election materials. See also below, section 3.2.

166   *Le Monde*, 21 nov. 1993; see also ibid., 20 nov. 1993. The French and Spanish governments declined to send observers, 'en raison "des conditions d'organization du scrutin, qui privent les élections de leur caractère vraiment pluraliste"...' Ibid., 24 nov. 1993.

167   See International Republican Institute, *Kenya: The December 29, 1992 Elections*, 1993, 32; National Election Monitoring Unit (NEMU), *The Multi-Party General Elections in Kenya*, 1993.

168   Commonwealth Observer Group, *Kenya 1992*, 39, 40. On the positive side, the Group noted the improvement in the performance of the Electoral Commission over time; a similar and ultimately more successful experience an opening up of the political system was recorded in Nicaragua in 1989-90: Freely Elected Heads, *Nicaragua 1989-90*, 12, 25-6.

Despite the fact that the whole electoral process cannot be given an unqualified rating as free and fair, the evolution of the process to polling day and the subsequent count was increasingly positive to a degree that we believe that the results in many instances directly reflect, however imperfectly, the expression of the will of the people. It constitutes a giant step on the road to multi-party democracy.

Whether such optimistic assessment will be borne out remains to be seen. One advantage of this approach may be that it facilitates the continuation of dialogue, and therefore also of pressure to bring national practice into line with international standards.[169]

3.1.8.1 Human rights and the election environment

A peaceful campaign, of course, is not solely the responsibility of the government. The tolerant climate in Bulgaria during the 1990 elections, for example, was attributed in large measure to the conduct of the political parties, which in turn was assisted by periodic meetings among party leaders at national and regional level.[170] Rallies were held generally without interference, although there were some incidents of damage to party buildings and campaign materials, and also of intimidation.[171] In Nicaragua, too, the parties moved quickly and effectively to quell pre-election violence, agreeing with outside help on a set of guidelines to bring it to an end.[172] Violence and harassment were particularly evident features of the 1990 election campaign in Pakistan, including murders, kidnapping and robberies.[173] Serious violence occurred again in 1993, although an

169   This also perhaps explains why the Commonwealth Observer Group were 'deeply saddened' by the opposition parties' rejection of the presidential election results in Ghana in 1992, despite their earlier commitment to accept them, and why they were encouraged by the hope that the parties would nonetheless choose to remain with the process and contest the parliamentary elections: *Ghana 1992*, 59-61.

170   NDI/NRI, *Bulgaria 1990*, 35-6. During the Cambodia elections in 1993, the UN likewise organized regular inter-party meetings, as a contribution to the resolution of disputes and reduction of friction. On Codes of Conduct, see further below, section 3.1.8.3.

171   Cf. NDI/Carter Center, *Zambia 1991*, 44-7.

172   Freely Elected Heads, *Nicaragua 1989-90*, 18.

173   NDI, *Pakistan 1990*, 52-4. The general election in Jamaica in March 1993 was also marred by violence, despite the code of conduct signed by political leaders committing all candidates to restrain their supporters: *Keesing's Record of World Events*, News Digest for March 1993, 39360. On violence in Kenya, see Commonwealth Observer Group, *Kenya 1992*, 23-4. The Group concluded that the Government could have made a greater effort to create a multi-party climate, and to promote greater public awareness and tolerance; in addition, all the parties could have done far more to control the worst excesses of their supporters: ibid., vii, x.

international observer delegation noted a significant improvement in the pre-election environment, compared to 1990. The government had sought to create an atmosphere in which the elections would be administered impartially, and the parties agreed that the government had succeeded in promoting an open, competitive process.[174]

The Joint International Observer Group (JIOG) in Malawi in 1993 for the national referendum noted that campaign conditions improved over time. To begin with, opposition activists found it difficult to hold meetings; permits were refused, or cancelled or only granted at the last minute; government party meetings, on the other hand, often gained priority or did not require permission. Some individuals were arrested and detained, and there were assaults, threats and intimidation, including failure by the police to intervene.[175] The JIOG invited all victims of harassment or intimidation to submit formal complaints in writing, and a number of serious, verified incidents were reported. Dismissals and arrests led the European Community to complain that the Malawi authorities had 'failed to reach acceptable standards of democratic campaigning..' Both sides at times also breached the prohibition of 'inflammatory, defamatory, or insulting' language. The general situation improved, however, as the campaign progressed.[176]

Violence and intimidation were major features of the 1990 elections in Romania, almost all of it directed against opposition members. Moreover, the government and incumbent president made 'no overt effort to help ensure a safe, tolerant and pluralistic campaign.'[177] Experience here provided a marked contrast to the peaceful conduct of elections in Czechoslovakia and Bulgaria.[178]

There may be cases of transition, for example, from war to peace, where, regrettably but realistically, higher levels of violence must be accepted as part of the movement towards representative democracy. In other situations, however, less tolerance may be due where a government

174   NDI Preliminary Statement. International Observer Delegation to the Pakistan National Elections, 8 Oct. 1993.

175   See also comment by the Inter-American Commission on Human Rights with respect to politically related human rights in Paraguay in 1987 and Panama in 1989: reports cited in *Final Report on Cases 9768, 9780 and 9828:* IACmHR, 97, paras. 56, 61. Above note 117.

176   JIOG, *Malawi 1993.*

177   Garber & Bjornlund, *New Democratic Frontier*, 83, 86f.

178   Ibid., at 125, 146. Likewise to that in Bangladesh in 1991: Commonwealth Observer Group, *Bangladesh 1991*, 28

fails to react promptly and effectively to violence and intimidation, thereby putting at issue its own commitment to an open, democratic process.[179]

3.1.8.2 Media access and coverage

Given that a choice between government and policy alternatives is central to the democratic ideal, access to the media in modern society is self-evidently crucial to the dissemination of party platforms and programmes. As the CSCE Copenhagen Document puts it, 'no legal or administrative obstacle (should stand) in the way of unimpeded access to the media on a non-discriminatory basis for all political groupings and individuals wishing to participate in the electoral process.'[180] Only if such facilities are available, will candidates effectively enjoy the right to express themselves freely, including by way of criticism,[181] and electors take the benefit of the freedom to seek and receive information.[182] Regrettably, the importance of these rights to the democratic and electoral process is only too well emphasized by the struggle to control media access, and by the abuse of such control, particularly in societies in transition, where broadcasting and newspapers have long been a government monopoly.[183]

The dangers of central control were nowhere more in evidence than in

---

179   The Inter-American Commission on Human Rights has noted that a government's connection to violence may 'modify the basic conditions of equality under which elections must be held': *Final Report on Cases 9768, 9780 and 9828:* IACmHR, 97, para. 74. Above note 117.

180   Para. (7.8), above section 2.6.

181   See *Oberschlick v. Austria*, Case No. 6/1990/197/257, European Court of Human Rights, 23 May 1991. The Court noted that freedom of the press afforded the public one of the best means of discovering and forming an opinion of the ideas and attitudes of political leaders. More generally, freedom of political debate was at the very core of the concept of a democratic society and the limits of acceptable criticism were accordingly wider with regard to a politician acting in his or her public capacity than in relation to a private individual.

182   Art. 19, 1966 Covenant on Civil and Political Rights; above, section 2.3. As the US delegate to the UN Third Committee noted in a related context in 1972: 'freedom of choice is indispensable to the exercise of the right of self-determination. For this freedom of choice to be meaningful, there must be corresponding freedom of thought, conscience, expression, movement and association. Self-determination entails legitimate, lively dissent and testing at the ballot box with frequent regularity.' Dept. of State Bulletin, 25 Dec. 1972, no. 1748.

183   The democratic process may also be threatened by excessive licence, where political issues and choices are overshadowed by personal attacks. The media in the 1992 Ghana elections were considered often to have overstepped the line between free speech and muck-raking; the idea of a 'Code of Conduct' for the media was suggested: Commonwealth Observer Group, *Ghana 1992*, 45-9; cf. Commonwealth Observer Group, *Guyana 1992*, Annex X, Guidelines for Media and Political Parties. See further below, section 3.1.8.3 and Annex 2.

the 1990 Romanian elections.[184] Even though the electoral law provided for television and radio time, the opposition,[185]

> suffered from limited access to programming, unpredictable placement and uneven access to recording studios and equipment...Television news coverage of the campaign was blatantly and consistently biased toward the Front...(and)... its bias constituted a major structural advantage..

The situation with respect to newspapers was no better; the supply of materials, printing facilities and the distribution network remained in government hands, and opposition parties were regularly intimidated to discourage publication.[186]

In other East European countries, media access and media activities were not always free from criticism, even if the margin of abuse never reached the same degree. In Hungary, for example, candidates repeatedly complained of uneven coverage, although access remained generally non-partisan.[187] In Bulgaria, new newspapers sprang up, but opposition papers tended to suffer from limited print-runs in government controlled facilities. Both television and state-owned newspapers did provide other than the 'official line', but as one commentator observed, 'given the realities of a transition period, the opposition never achieved full equality in their ability to use the media.'[188] In Czechoslovakia, all parties were granted four hours each of free radio and television time, and placement was determined

---

184 'The campaign was systematically unfair. The Front enjoyed all the advantages of having assumed the reins of an absolutist state and exploited these advantages to the maximum. The opposition suffered from a lack of every possible resource...': Carothers, T., 'Romania', in Garber & Bjornlund, *New Democratic Frontier*, 83.

185 Ibid., at 84.

186 Ibid. See also US Commission, *Central and Eastern Europe*, 110-11.

187 US Commission, *Central and Eastern Europe*, at 38f; also Melia, T.O., 'Hungary,' in Garber & Bjornlund, *New Democratic Frontier*, 54-5.

188 Garber, L., 'Bulgaria,' in Garber & Bjornlund, *New Democratic Frontier*, 148. Cf. CSCE Office for Democratic Institutions and Human Rights, 'International Observation of the Referendum held in the Russian Federation on April 25, 1993': political parties had had roughly equal possibilities to convey their views to the electorate. The printed media reflected a broad spectrum of views; the electronic media, mostly in pro-Government hands, allowed significant time to opposition viewpoints. The CSCE report nevertheless recommended a law on access by political parties to state-run television and radio during an election campaign.

by a computer-generated random schedule.[189]

Media coverage was problematic in the referendum campaign in Malawi, given the monopoly of the Malawi Broadcasting Corporation (MBC). The MBC provided extensive coverage to the President, but little to multi-party advocates. Programming was unbalanced at the beginning of the campaign, and did not maintain the neutrality or equality of treatment required by the referendum regulations. Presidential rally broadcasts also tended to take precedence, even over civic education programmes. The main newspaper, the *Daily Times*, was government-owned, and opposition newspapers could not compete, although a ban on two papers was lifted after a court order. Campaigning by opposition groups was made more difficult by the lack of transport facilities and organizational experience, and by unequal access to campaigning basics, such as public address systems.

Reviewing the Senegalese electoral code in 1991, the NDI recommended that an 'equitable formula', which might take account of media strength and track record, 'should be devised that ensures all parties an adequate opportunity to communicate their positions to the electorate through the media.'[190] In its preliminary review of the 1993 Senegalese presidential elections, the NDI noted that media access had considerably improved, but that state-controlled media tended to favour the incumbent.[191] Article 36 of the UN Electoral Law for Cambodia and UN practice leading up to the 1993 elections provide an international perspective on the principle of media access. The law stipulated that to ensure fair access to the media for all political parties contesting the election, all newspapers and

189   For comment, see Carnahan, R. and Corley, J., 'Czechoslovakia,' in Garber & Bjornlund, *New Democratic Frontier*, 126-7. Cf. the situation in the Cameroon, where broadcasting time was divided among the parties on the basis of the number of candidates running. News coverage, however, was unevenly balanced in favour of the president: NDI, *Cameroon 1992*, 30-3. For an assessment of the media role in Zambia, see Commonwealth Observer Group, *Zambia 1991*, 10, noting that both parties had a fair chance to present their message in the government controlled media; NDI/Carter Center, *Zambia 1991*, 41-3. See also, NDI, *Pakistan 1990*, 49-52, 113-4; NDI Preliminary Statement. International Observer Delegation to the Pakistan National Elections, 8 October 1993, noting that the electronic media had provided generally balanced coverage and also access for some twenty-two parties to present their message directly to the people. The printed media was also accessible, and enjoyed freedom in political reporting. Cf. Commonwealth Observer Group, *Malaysia 1990*, 13-16 (balanced picture not available because of denial of adequate coverage of opposition personalities and policies); Commonwealth Observer Group, *Kenya 1992*, 26-7, 39 (lack of a free press was evident; state-owned broadcasting media were partisan).

190   NDI, *Senegal 1991*, 30-1.

191   National Democratic Institute for International Affairs. 'Executive Summary. February 21, 1993 Presidential Elections in Senegal.' International Delegation Report. Washington, D.C. 1993.

broadcasting media controlled by public authorities should be made available to the UN at no cost, for the purpose of publicity and electoral education. Attempts to block access were resisted by the United Nations Transitional Authority in Cambodia (UNTAC), which also organized special television panels at which party representatives were able to air their policies. In addition, UNTAC's own radio transmitting 15 hours daily was made available on an equal basis to all parties contesting the election.[192] An October 1993 decree in Russia provided for equal access to the mass media, especially the state-owned radio and television networks, for all candidates and parties. In the lead-in to the December elections, both networks allocated one hour per night, with the order of appearance decided by lottery.[193] Although equal time was given, however, the news coverage was reported as generally pro-government.[194]

The principle of equal access to the media is widely accepted in established democracies. The formulae may vary, but the underlying premise is the same: those competing in an election should have a reasonable opportunity to get their message across. Danish radio and television guidelines, for example, assure *equal access* to all registered parties, and *equal time*, regardless of the size of the party; paid advertisements on radio and television, however, are not allowed.[195] In France, radio and television time is divided equally between majority and opposition parties, although parties not represented in the legislature receive only seven minutes airtime.[196] In the United Kingdom and Ireland, television and radio time is decided by committees comprising the broadcasting authorities and the parties, but again paid advertisements are not permitted, other than in the press and on hoardings.[197] Ireland has a statutory requirement of fairness, objectivity and impartiality with respect to radio and television, but not the press.[198] In the United Kingdom,

192   See IPU, 'Report of IPU Election Observer Mission, Cambodia, 16 May-4 June 1993,' Geneva, (1993), 7-8
193   US Commission, *Russia 1993*, 10, 17.
194   Ibid., 17.
195   ECPRD, *Electoral System Legislation*, 62. See also *Wilson v. Independent Broadcasting Authority* (1979) S.L.T. 279; although three out of four political parties supported devolution in a Scottish referendum, the court ruled that broadcasting time should be allocated equally to both sides of the question. Cited in Merloe, below note 199, 83.
196   Ibid., 259; also Masclet, *Droit électoral*, 232-4.
197   ECPRD, *Electoral System Legislation*, 303-4, 476-7.
198   Ibid. Private media are frequently problematic. The linkage of major newspapers to the government has long given rise to concern in Mexico, as has biased reporting by the principal television stations: Freely Elected Heads, *Reform in Mexico*, 7.

candidates may take part in election campaign programmes about their constituencies, only if all their rival candidates either also take part or agree that the programme can go ahead.

Access and fair and balanced coverage are thus the two main issues, with the 'appropriateness' of paid advertising finding different responses, both in established and emergent democracies.[199] In a recent decision, the Australian High Court considered different perspectives when it held that a provision prohibiting all paid political advertising in the electronic media to be unconstitutional.[200] The prohibition violated the implicit protection of freedom of political communication because, in particular, it also allowed free airtime to be allocated to political parties in such a way as to give an unfair advantage to incumbent candidates and parties represented in the previous legislature; no provision was made for organizations and associations to have paid or unpaid access to the electronic media. In its judgment, the Court indicated that the prohibition of paid political advertisements would probably be upheld, if part of a package ensuring fair access for all political players.

A recent review of election broadcasting proposes some sixteen guidelines, drawing on international human rights law and prevailing practice among established democracies.[201] Among those classified as mandatory are the obligation of government media to inform the public, to grant access and accord unbiased coverage, to abolish or suspend restrictions on public comment, to punish attacks on media personnel, to refrain from censorship, to grant access on a non-discriminatory basis to all parties, to ensure balance and fairness, to provide education for voters, and to provide for judicial review of broadcasting-related decisions. A comprehensive and structured approach to such influential media is clearly called for, if electors are to understand the choices available.

3.1.8.3 Codes of Conduct

Codes of Conduct agreed between the parties are increasingly accepted in potentially tense situations as a practical basis for contributing to a peaceful

---

199 See generally Merloe, P., *Election Campaign Broadcasting in Transitional Democracies: Problems, Principles and Guidelines.* Prepared for Article 19, the International Centre against Censorship. Pre-publication draft. August 1993.

200 *Australian Capital Television Pty. Ltd. v. The Commonwealth; New South Wales v. The Commonwealth (No. 2)* (1992) 66 A.L.J.R. 695, discussed in Merloe, above note, at pp. 16-19.

201 See Merloe, P., *Election Campaign Broadcasting in Transitional Democracies: Problems, Principles and Guidelines,* 1993, 61-84.

election; in the long term, such codes may also help to develop confidence in the democratic process as a mechanism for implementing representative government and effecting peaceful change. Article 7 of the Elections Annex to the *Comprehensive Settlement Agreement* for Cambodia, for example, provided that 'Adherence to a Code of Conduct established by UNTAC in consultation with the SNC (Supreme National Council of Cambodia) will be a condition for...participation' in the elections. The Code laid down the basic campaign freedoms to be enjoyed by all parties, but also repeatedly stressed the prohibition of intimidation, violence and possession of weapons at political meetings. The parties agreed to advise UNTAC of planned rallies and, in co-operation and liaison with the UN, to avoid coinciding with meetings by other parties. All parties also undertook, in effect, to educate their supporters in the meaning of democracy, for example, by emphasizing the secrecy of the ballot and that no one will ever know how an individual has voted.

Perhaps the most important element in the Code for Cambodia was the arrangement that all parties should meet at least once every two weeks with the UN Chief Electoral Officer, to discuss any matters of concern arising in the campaign. By thus establishing a regular channel of communication between the parties, the UN was able to anticipate and avoid incidents and misunderstandings that might otherwise have led to violence.[202]

Other Codes of Conduct have followed a similar direction. That adopted in Ghana in October 1992, for example, included a provision whereby the losing candidates undertook to concede defeat on the Electoral Commission declaring a free and fair election. The Seychelles Code included a section dealing with conduct relating to posters and banners, while guidelines adopted for Guyana's 1992 election specifically focused on the media and political parties.

A crucial problem in transition situations is often the failure of competing parties to communicate with each other, together with a lack of confidence in the ability of the system to produce a free and fair result. Codes of Conduct, in which the parties agree on the basic ground rules and

---

202   For comment on the Cambodia experience, see IPU, *Report of IPU Election Observer Mission, Cambodia, 16 May-4 June 1993*, Geneva, (1993); for text of the Code of Conduct, see ibid., Annex II, and below, Annex 2, which also provides other examples of such Codes of Conduct drawn from the following observer delegation reports: Commonwealth Observer Group, *Bangladesh 1991*, Annex 7; *Ghana 1992*, Annex XVII; *Guyana 1992*, Annex X (Guidelines for Media and Political Parties); *Seychelles November 1992*, Annex VII.

to meet regularly during the campaign period, clearly contribute not only to the avoidance of potentially dangerous confrontation, but also to popular support for the democratic process.

3.1.9 Balloting, monitoring and results

Although the fairness of any election is unlikely to be determined solely by reference to what happens on election day, the actual process of balloting deserves particular attention. Among other issues, balloting raises the question of the location of polling stations, and their accessibility for the population; the presence of competent officials, versed in the procedure; the presence of party representatives; secrecy of the act of voting and the security of the ballot box; the integrity of the counting process and its translation into a genuine political result. Broken down still further, balloting also involves the organization and management of voting, including the opening and closing of polling stations at stated times; the arrangement of booths and the orderly movement of voters; the identification and verification of voters (hence the importance of a credible registration system, discussed above); an established procedure for objection and challenge; the issue of ballot papers to recognized voters; the marking of ballot papers out of sight of officials or other electors; the deposit of marked ballots; and, in the absence of other sufficient guarantees, the identification of voters, for example, with indelible ink, in order to prevent double voting. The counting process in turn requires measures to ensure that ballot boxes are empty before voting begins, that they are secure when polling stations are closed, or during any period of transit,[203] and that votes are tallied in a process that inspires confidence in the electorate.

The fundamental rules relating to the exercise of electoral rights centre on non-discrimination, access to the poll and the act of voting, equal and universal suffrage, secret ballot and guarantees that the results of the vote shall reflect the free expression of the will of the electors. The present discussion is limited to these critical issues, referring back where appropriate to earlier comment.

203   During its observation of the Cambodia election in 1993, the IPU delegation followed up reports that ballot box seals had broken during transit to safe areas. After inspecting the seals and witnessing transport conditions, it expressed its satisfaction that the breaking had been accidental (largely because of the quality of the seals, coupled with the equally poor road conditions), that UNTAC had taken prompt corrective measures, and that there was no evidence to suggest that the ballot had been affected in any way or that any party had gained as a result. *Report of IPU Election Observer Mission, Cambodia, 16 May-4 June 1993*, paras. 38-41, 57.

First, the international legal principle of *non-discrimination* requires that no one shall be denied or prejudiced in the exercise of rights for reasons considered irrelevant, such as race, colour, sex, language, religion, political or other opinion, national or social origin, birth or other status. This principle touches practically every aspect of the electoral process, from registration onwards. It is explicit in the principle of universal suffrage, discussed above, and inherent in the right to have access both to the 'machinery' of voting (the electoral roll, voting materials), and to the polling both itself. Access here means not only physical access, in the sense of freedom from violence or intimidation,[204] or from obstruction by police or extra-government forces; but also accessibility, in the sense that polling booths should be so sited that voters do not have to travel far.[205]

The principle of *equal suffrage*, described above,[206] also requires that no vote shall have greater value than any other vote. This touches on constituency delimitation, but also has practical implications at the polling station level, in that measures must be taken to guard against multiple voting, by scrupulously checking voter cards, marking voters with indelible ink, or both.

The *secrecy of the ballot* is one aspect of the process which permits of scarcely any qualification. Once considered just one of several 'equivalent free voting procedures',[207] the secret ballot now stands alone and absolute, and is frequently elevated to the level of constitutional law or protected by other statutory rules.[208] The few remaining contrary instances are either on the wane or must be appreciated in their particular historical context.

The principle ran into 'traditional' objections in Senegal, where a secret vote was available as an option, but the practice of *not* using a voting booth

204 During the elections in New Caledonia in 1988, roadblocks prevented access to several *bureaux de vote*, and violence also took place. Fourteen bureaux could not open, and three others could not remain open for the full voting period. The *Conseil constitutionnel* annulled the votes from three *bureaux*, but given the national character of the ballot, considered that though they were serious, the incidents in question were not sufficient to justify invalidating the election as a whole: Masclet, *Droit électoral*, 268-9.

205 A guiding principle in Ghana's 1992 elections and Malawi's 1993 referendum was that no one should have to travel more than 5 kilometres to vote: Commonwealth Observer Group, *Ghana 1992;* JIOG, *Malawi 1993*.

206 Described above, section 3.1.2.

207 Compare art. 21(c), Universal Declaration of Human Rights and art. 25(b), 1966 Covenant on Civil and Political Rights.

208 Cf. art. 3(3), Constitution of France: 'Le suffrage peut être direct ou indirect dans les conditions prévues par la Constitution. Il est toujours universel, égal et *secret*'. Cited in Masclet, *Droit électoral*, 270.

was widely accepted. Opposition critics argued that this very practice itself created pressure to vote publicly in such a way as not to display disloyalty to government.[209] NDI in turn recommended that a mandatory secret ballot be instituted, which came into effect for the first time in the 1993 presidential elections.[210] Similar concerns have emerged in Kenya, Nigeria and Uganda. The 1988 election in Kenya involved the 'public queuing system' at the key primary level, under which voters publicly lined up behind photographs of their preferred candidate. Critics at the time noted that the intimidation inherent in this process was amply confirmed by the results, in which no candidate critical of the ruling party or of government policies was selected.[211] A secret ballot was in principle required for the 1992 elections in Kenya, but in practice it was often compromised by poor layout of polling stations, inadequate screens and insufficient management of voting streams. The process for marking the ballots of illiterate voters in the presence of all party agents also re-opened the way to a public voting system, especially in rural areas where large numbers of voters were illiterate.[212]

A related issue to involve the UN Electoral Assistance Unit in the preparations for Malawi's national referendum concerned the use of one or two ballot boxes. The government initially proposed a system of separate

209   The discouragement of such 'public voting' and the preservation of the principle and practice of the secret ballot explain why ballots that allow the elector to be identified are frequently considered null and void. Cf. Masclet, *Droit électoral*, 272, 295-6.

210   NDI, *Senegal 1991*, 33-4; National Democratic Institute for International Affairs. 'Executive Summary, February 21, 1993 Presidential Elections in Senegal.' International Delegation Report. Washington, D.C. 1993. 'Public voting' still prevails in parts of Switzerland, one of the oldest-established democracies, and is the reason why that country has not so far ratified Protocol 1 of the European Convention on Human Rights. The *Landesgemeinde* is the supreme authority in five Swiss cantons, comprising an assembly of all active citizens meeting from time to time to deliberate affairs of state, to elect and to vote on legislative proposals. Although varying in detail from canton to canton, the *Landesgemeinde* combine electoral and legislative functions, in which voting takes place by show of hands. For comment, see Villiger, M.E., *Handbuch der Europäischer Menschenrechtskonvention (EMRK)*, Zurich, 1993, §33; Schweizer, R.J., 'Zur Stellung der Schweiz gegenüber Art. 3 der Zusatzprotokolls zur Europäischer Menschenrechtskonvention (Gewährleistung von freien und geheimen Wahlen), 41; Grisel, E., *Initiative et Référendum Populaires: Traité de la démocratie semi-directe en droit Suisse*, Dorigny, 1987, section VI.

211   See Department of State, *Country Reports on Human Rights Practices for 1988*, 155-68 (1989), describing the practice; and Human Rights Watch and Lawyers Committee for Human Rights, *Critique: Review of the Department of State's Country Reports on Human Rights Practices for 1988*, 99-104 (1989), noting the inadequacy of the Department's criticism. Parliamentary elections in Nigeria in 1992 used the same voting system; the voter turnout of only 25 per cent was attributed in part to hostility to the 'open ballot': Inter-Parliamentary Union, *Chronicle of Parliamentary Elections and Developments*, No. 27, 1992-1993, 170. On Uganda, see ibid., No. 23, 1989-1990, 123.

212   Commonwealth Observer Group, *Kenya 1992*, 34-5.

boxes: rather than marking a ballot, the voter places a ballot in whatever box represents the desired choice, thus making voting easier for a largely illiterate population. The UN, however, argued for a single box, on the ground that if voting is done in secret, one or other of two boxes may be easily stuffed with extra ballots or tampered with in other ways. With the agreement of the government, an outside expert was brought in, who in turn proposed the use of a single ballot box and two ballot papers, representing the two choices. The system had been successfully used in Mali, Guinea, Senegal and Eritrea, and was accepted by the government.[213]

The question of secrecy also came up in Bulgaria in 1990, in one area because of the transparency of the ballot envelopes, in another because of the composition or placement of polling booths.[214] Similar complaints were heard in Romania, where election officials were also seen to 'help' voters inside the booths.[215] The number of irregularities there and in Cameroon,[216] even if not 'systematic', contributed to the overall lack of confidence in the electoral process. The many values of secrecy include, in particular, the fact that it ensures the freedom of the elector, who is able to choose free of all pressure:[217]

> Le moyen le plus efficace de préserver la liberté de l'électeur est bien d'éviter que le sens de son vote ne soit connu: ainsi il n'est plus tenu par les promesses ou engagements qui lui auraient été indûment extorgués et il est à l'abri des menaces de ceux à qui son vote déplairait et qui pourraient avoir prise sur lui.

The record of electoral balloting nevertheless also contains many examples of impartial management by election officials, effective voting by electors familiar with the system and the requirements, and an effective process made transparent by the presence of party representatives, or poll

---

213   JIOG, *Malawi 1993*.
214   NDI/NRI, *Bulgaria 1990*, 45-6.
215   Carothers, T., 'Romania', in Garber & Bjornlund, *New Democratic Frontier*, 90: 'Given the tradition of surveillance and political repression...the lack of secrecy may have had a chilling effect on those contemplating voting for the opposition.' See also the concerns expressed by the Council of Europe delegation to the Sept. 1992 elections: CE Doc. 6724, Add. V, pp. 8-9 (1 Feb. 1993).
216   NDI, *Cameroon 1992*, 36-41.
217   Masclet, *Droit électoral*, 270.

watchers.[218] In France, each candidate may appoint one or more delegates who are authorised to be permanently present in places where the election is being held. Their job is to monitor electoral operations and to ensure that the *bureau de vote* functions correctly. At the count, they are called on to sign the record of the proceedings, to which they may add their own comments.[219] In the United Kingdom, those present include the presiding officer (who is in charge), polling clerks, on-duty police, the candidates, election agents and polling agents.[220]

International observers have repeatedly stressed the importance of monitors in building voter confidence and ensuring the integrity of the system. In Bulgaria, for example, representatives from at least two parties monitored the balloting at nearly every polling station. In addition, a non-partisan, civic organization, the Bulgarian Association for Fair Elections (BAFE) was present; and it was the *absence* of such monitors in Romania that helped to reduce voter confidence. Reviewing the 1993 national referendum in Malawi, the JIOG report concluded that 'Domestic monitors are an important key to the fairness of any election. They are a check against errors, misconduct and fraud...their very presence should limit opportunities for wrong doing.'[221] The duties of such monitors, as described in the report, show the practical ways in which a representative presence can build public confidence by ensuring that the polling station arrangement is correct and that the ballot box empty and sealed before voting; checking against the impersonation of voters; checking that no one is denied the right to vote without cause; ensuring that the vote is truly secret; watching for unexpected problems; participating in decisions that require a departure from the rules, for example, on the need for additional boxes; preventing campaigning and intimidation around polling stations and in queues; ensuring that the polling station is correctly closed and that no one is prevented from voting; observing the count and agreeing on or challenging difficult decisions, for example, with respect to void or damaged ballots; and receiving a signed copy of the count, as a check on any tampering with ballots or with the result between the polling station

218   For examples and descriptions of procedure, see JIOG, *Malawi 1993*; NDI Preliminary Statement. International Observer Delegation to the Pakistan National Elections, 8 October 1993; NDI/Carter Center, *Zambia 1991*, 52-3 (noting minor irregularities); NDI/NRI, *Bulgaria 1990*, 42-6; US Commission, *Central and Eastern Europe*, 40-2 (Hungary).
219   Masclet, *Droit électoral*, 279.
220   ECPRD, *Electoral System Legislation*, 487ff.
221   JIOG, *Malawi 1993*, para. 124.

and the district centre.[222]

States participating in the CSCE Copenhagen Meeting in 1990 expressed their view that 'the presence of observers, both foreign and domestic, can enhance the electoral process...They therefore invite observers from any other CSCE participating States and any appropriate private institutions and organizations who may wish to do so to observe the course of their national election proceedings, to the extent permitted by law.' Despite the openness to outside presence, foreign observers run the risk of controversy, either because they are perceived as interfering, or because they do their job too well, or not at all.[223] Still, a considerable body of knowledge is now available to ensure that the job is well done. As one experienced commentator has observed,[224]

> a trustworthy election system is critical to ensuring the existence of a democratic form of government. When questions arise regarding the quality of the system, governments and nongovernmental organizations should be prepared to sponsor international observer delegations that can then determine whether a commitment to free and fair elections exists and, where appropriate, encourage ways to improve the electoral process.

Effective *local* monitors, either party representatives or recognized impartial officials, appear more likely to satisfy national aspirations for a free and fair electoral system. In situations of transition, however, national institutions may well be best developed and strengthened by remaining accessible to international observers and receptive to training and education programmes.

Finally, there is the *count* and, in appropriate cases, the *transfer of power* to the successful party in the election. Complementary to the

---

222 Ibid. In its 1991 review of the Senegalese electoral code, the NDI recommended that the presence of party representatives as poll watchers be facilitated; this seems to have been achieved for the 1993 elections, at least for the balloting phase, if not for voter registration: Executive Summary, February 21, 1993 Presidential Elections in Senegal, April 8, 1993.

223 For some of the possible difficulties, see NDI/Carter Center, *Zambia 1991*, 47-50, 61-5, 66-7; also Pierre Cornillon, Secretary General, Inter-Parliamentary Union, 'Rights and Responsibilities of Election Observers,' paper presented to the International Conference of La Laguna on Freedom of Elections and the International Observation of Elections, Tenerife, 27 Feb.-2 Mar. 1994. In Mexico, outside observers are still viewed with suspicion; domestic observers may be tolerated as individuals, but only under strict conditions: Freely Elected Heads, *Electoral Reform in Mexico*, 31.

224 Garber, L., 'The Role of International Observers,' in Garber & Bjornlund, *New Democratic Frontier*, 211, 220.

principle of secret ballot is the integrity of the count, which looks both to ensure that the expressed wish of the elector is taken into account, and that the result declared corresponds with the totality of the votes cast. Sometimes, the ballots will be counted on the spot, and on others, the ballot boxes are transported to central or regional counting stations. In either cases, transparency of process is as valuable as accuracy in counting. Transportation of ballot boxes commonly gives rise to fear of substitution, as happened in Panama in 1989; on the other hand, not to undertake central counting may lead, for example, to a small community being identified as having voted one way or the other, with a resulting possibility of prejudice in any later distribution of national resources.[225] Again, confidence in the process can be enhanced by the presence of party representatives both at the count and during any interim period of transport.

Parallel voting tabulation has also proven its value as a means of independently verifying the results reported by electoral authorities. In this process, monitors record results obtained from selected polling sites, and compare them with the official results:[226]

> The monitoring of vote counts as part of an overall election-observation effort can boost the confidence of voters suspicious of possible fraud, permit results to be projected more quickly than the official results, and allow for the identification of actual winners and the consequent exposure of any attempted manipulations.

In addition, as experience in Nicaragua in 1990 suggests, an early appreciation of the probable results obtained through parallel vote tabulation may help observers facilitate a peaceful transfer of power, through informed contacts with incumbent and opposition leaders.[227]

3.1.10 Complaints and dispute resolution

A free and fair electoral system depends not only on voter registration, free campaigning, monitors and secret ballots; it must also be able to deal promptly and effectively with the different types of complaint that will inevitably arise. These might include refusal of the right to stand as a

225   Commonwealth Observer Group, *Zambia 1991*, 18-19.
226   See generally Garber, L. and Cowan, G., 'The Virtues of Parallel Vote Tabluations,' 4 *Journal of Democracy* 95, 106 (1993).
227   Freely Elected Heads, *Nicaragua 1989-1990*, 25-6.

candidate or to vote, attempts to suppress voter turn-out,[228] alleged misinterpretation of the electoral laws or procedures, alleged violations of the criminal law, disputes regarding the accuracy of the count, or claims that the cumulative effect of such irregularities is so extensive as to invalidate the elections.[229] Generally, what is at issue is either the validity of the result, or the penalization of those who have violated electoral laws. The right to a remedy for violation of human rights is itself a human right,[230] while sanctions against those who infringe the provisions of the electoral law are implicitly required in any effective system of implementation. The integrity of the system requires not only that such issues be dealt with by an independent and impartial authority, such as the electoral commission or the courts, but also that decisions be reached in a timely manner, in order that the outcome of elections not be delayed. As with other aspects of the electoral process, the availability of such procedures must be open and known to the electorate and the parties.

Part of the process for anticipating and dealing with complaints includes much of what has been said above, including such practices as monitors and parallel vote tablulations. At the formal level, what is important is not so much the sanction, as the timeliness of the response. In cases of violence or intimidation, for example, what is needed is a prompt reaction, in order that continuing disturbances not interfere with the elector's essential freedom to choose. The tendency is for national systems also to try to deal expeditiously with errors of form, however. The ultimate objective remains that of establishing representative government, and the national interest is generally perceived as best met by the speedy resolution of potentially divisive issues.

3.2 Evaluation

Determining whether an election is genuine and free and fair involves more than assessing whether electors turn up to vote; it requires a judgment on a

228 See Thomas B. Edsall and Malcolm Gladwell, 'Probe Begins on NJ "Vote Suppressing" Claim,' *The Guardian Weekly*, 21 Nov. 1993, p. 14 (from the *Washington Post*), reporting allegations that the campaign of Republican New Jersey Governor-elect Christine Todd Whitman spent hundreds of thousands of dollars to suppress black voter turnout, using 'walking around money' to persuade African-American ministers and Democratic ward and precinct workers not to engage in get-out-the-vote activities.

229 Cf. NDI/NRI, *Bulgaria 1990*, 53-4.

230 See, for example, art. 2(3), 1966 Covenant on Civil and Political Rights; art. 13, 1950 European Convention on Human Rights; art. 25, 1969 American Convention on Human Rights; art. 7, 1986 African Charter on Human and Peoples' Rights.

dynamic and often evolving process, which itself often demands to be seen as a critical, if somewhat imperfect step in the direction of representative democracy. Many of the elections considered above left observers making 'on the one hand/on the other hand' assessments.[231] Each election was affected by local circumstances and the nation's particular historical moment, but together they have added to the repository of State practice from which international standards emerge or consolidate.

Observer experience is no less important when an election fails to meet those standards, and yet is not subject to overt manipulation. In Pakistan in 1990, the NDI's post-election review found that observers had confronted relatively few incidents of serious irregularity.[232] By that time, however, the opposition had already denounced the elections for 'massive fraud'; in the absence of concrete evidence, the international observer delegation refrained from condemning the elections, only thereby to lay itself open to the charge of failing to certify their fraudulent character:[233]

> ...the media and policymakers desire unequivocal evaluations of elections. However, the reality is that such evaluations sometimes are not possible, particularly when only some of the allegations can be corroborated and the cumulative effect of the irregularities on the process requires subjective judgments...Observer delegations in these circumstances should simply report the allegations and their observations, without necessarily addressing the ultimate question of whether the elections were or were not free and fair.

Putting the varied experience of international observer delegations, United Nations electoral assistance activities, and national laws and practices together with the existing rules and standards of international law allows

231   See, for example, Garber, L., 'Bulgaria', in Garber & Bjornlund, *New Democratic Frontier*, at 145: 'A final evaluation of the election campaign in Bulgaria...requires analyzing the extent to which all parties were able to communicate their messages and the degree to which the government affirmatively acted to eliminate inequities in the process. On the positive side, the campaign featured a broad spectrum of active parties; no legal or practical impediment prevented any political party from forming or competing in the elections. On the negative side was the disparity in resources available to the parties.' Garber later notes that absolute equality of opportunities for political parties, or even relative balance, is seldom possible: ibid., at 156.

232   NDI, *Pakistan 1990*, 80-1; see also NDI, *Cameroon 1992*, 52-5.

233   Ibid., 103-9, at 108; for the delegation's recommendations, see at 110-7. Cf. the assessment of the role of international and domestic observers in NDI/Carter Center, *Zambia 1991*, 67-9. See also the assessment by the Commonwealth Observer Group of the 1992 Kenya elections: above note 168 and accompanying text.

for a reasonably coherent statement of the requirements for free and fair elections within today's system of inter-dependent States. Many key questions are as yet unanswered, including the extent to which, and 'against' whom, a people may claim a right to representative government, or the lawful extent of the international community's interest in every State's electoral process.

The following section presents those rules and principles which, on the basis of the above review, can be considered as possessing an absolute or near-absolute character. To these are attached other standards, many of which have been shown to contribute to the effective realisation of the goals set by general international law. In each case, the rules, principles and standards in question appear to reflect a broad consensus of opinion among both established and emerging democracies, the only distinction being the degree to which one or other may reflect a positive obligation, rather than a desirable standard or practice.

4. INTERNATIONAL STANDARDS

International law sets specific objectives with respect to the holding of periodic free and fair elections, and lays down a variety of related obligations. Principally if not exclusively obligations of conduct, they leave States to decide how, in their particular political, cultural and historical context, the objectives may be best achieved. A margin of appreciation, however, is not the same as complete freedom of choice, and even where there is discretion, international law sets certain conditioning parameters. For example, the principle of non-discrimination excludes a number of disenfranchising measures, while confining and structuring choices regarding constituency delimitation and the relative weight of voting power, both considered in the light of the complementary principles of representation by population and equal suffrage. The rule with respect to the secret ballot crosses from an obligation of result to one of conduct; alternatives are *not* allowed. Instead, the State is bound to take such steps as are necessary to ensure not only that secrecy is observed and maintained, but also that the integrity of the choice so made is protected in the count that follows and in the implementation of the result.

Fundamental human rights, for example, to hold and express opinions, to receive and share information, as well as freedom of movement, association and assembly, all give specific content to, and thus limit, the choices open to States in the regulation of an electoral campaign. If the will of the people is to find expression in a genuine election involving policies and representatives, then human rights must be effectively respected and protected so as to allow an informed choice to be made; only the narrowest of limitations are permitted, commensurate with what is necessary in a democratic society and with the paramount consideration of ensuring that the election reflects the will of the people.[1]

The choices made by the State are thus to be applied so that they are *effective*, that is, oriented to the objective of a free and fair election; and in such a way as to take account of other obligations in the field of human rights. Complementary principles of reasonableness and proportionality operate at the same time, to show when and where State choices, including

---

1   At times, there will evidently be tension between one's appreciation of the needs of a democratic society and of what must be tolerated in order to ensure a free and fair election. These issues are by no means new in the human rights context, however, and are capable of objectively justifiable resolution without resort to overriding theories of national security.

omissions, fail to meet international requirements.

Obligations in international law are not generally self-executing—they need *implementation* at the domestic level. The complexities and inter-relationships between electoral rights and objectives seem clearly to require a statutory framework and appropriate machinery, but neither universal nor regional human rights instruments contain any formal obligation to enact electoral legislation. The practical choices open to States in meeting their international obligations are not unlimited, however, and certain means are increasingly preferred. Article 2(2) of the 1966 Covenant on Civil and Political Rights, for example, provides that 'Where not already provided for by existing legislative or other measures, each State Party...undertakes to take the necessary steps, in accordance with its constitutional processes and with the provisions of the present Covenant, to adopt such legislative or other measures as may be necessary to give effect to the rights recognized...' The objective of free and fair elections, with its foundation both in the recognition of individual rights and in the existence of regular and open procedures, limits the range of options. Legislation can thus be considered *essential* to establish the country-specific scheme of representation, to identify applicable human rights and their beneficiaries, such as who may vote, and to ensure the availability of effective remedies. It is not the final answer, however, for neither freedom nor fairness can simply be legislated into every corner of the electoral process.

From an international law perspective, what counts is what finally results, and a tradition of free and fair elections must be maintained and consolidated over the long-term. To this extent, election obligations and the goal of representative democracy have a *programmatic* dimension, anticipating progress in building democratic institutions, strengthening the confidence of the people in the democratic process, and leading to better and more democratic government. In the furtherance of these aims, therefore, States should

- □ **take the necessary legislative steps to establish the rights and institutional framework for periodic and genuine free and fair elections, in accordance with their obligations under international law; and**

☐ **take the necessary policy and institutional steps to ensure the progressive achievement and consolidation of democratic goals.**

This review of State practice, considered together with and as contributing to the governing rules and principles, suggests the following minimum international law standards applicable to elections which, for the purposes of summary classification, can be divided into three categories: (1) the goal or objective set by international law; (2) the rights and responsibilities of individuals and political parties or groups; and (3) the combination of specific duties, programmatic obligations, responsibilities and entitlements incumbent on the State.

4.1 The Goal or Objective

International law's goal and the means by which it should be achieved can be stated quite simply: Every State should be possessed of a government whose authority derives from the will of the people as expressed by secret ballot in genuine free and fair elections held at regular intervals on the basis of universal and equal suffrage.

4.2 The Rights & Responsibilities of Individuals & Political Parties

In their law and practice, States must recognize and make provision for:

☐ **the right of the individual to vote, on a non-discriminatory basis, in parliamentary elections**

☐ **the right of the individual to access an effective, impartial and non-discriminatory procedure for the registration of voters**

☐ **the right of every eligible citizen to be registered as a voter, subject only to disqualification in accordance with clear criteria established by law, that are objectively verifiable and not subject to arbitrary decision**

☐ **the right of the individual whose right to vote or to be registered is negatively affected by an action or omission of the State or its officials to have access to a procedure competent to review such measures or to correct such errors promptly and effectively**

- ☐ the right of the individual to have equal and effective access to a polling station in order to exercise his or her right to vote
- ☐ the right of the individual to exercise his or her right equally with others and to have his or her vote accorded equivalent weight to that of others
- ☐ the right of the individual to vote in secret, which right shall not be restricted in any manner whatsoever, and to respect for the integrity of his or her choice
- ☐ the right of the individual to present himself or herself as a candidate for election

In addition, individuals enjoy rights of association, for example, to establish or join political parties; and, together with such political parties, they in turn enjoy campaign and related rights. States therefore must provide for the following:

- ☐ the right of the individual to join, or together with others to establish, a political party for the purpose of competing in an election
- ☐ the right to express political opinions without interference otherwise than as permitted under international law
- ☐ the right to seek, receive and impart information and to make an informed choice
- ☐ the right to move freely within the country in order to campaign for election
- ☐ the right to campaign on an equal basis with other political parties, including the party representing the existing government
- ☐ the right to have access to the media, particularly the electronic media, in order to put forward their political views
- ☐ the right of candidates, political parties and party members to security with respect to their lives and property
- ☐ the right to the protection of the law and to a remedy for violation of political and electoral rights

Electoral and political rights carry responsibilities to the community; national legislation should also recognize,

□ the obligation of the individual and of political parties not to engage in or incite violence
□ the obligation of candidates, political parties and party members to respect the rights and freedoms of others
□ the obligation of candidates, political parties and party members to accept the outcome of a free and fair election

4.3   The Rights and Responsibilities of Government

Experience and recent State practice confirm the necessity for oversight of the electoral process, for institutionalized responsibility for implementation by impartial election officials, and for civic education. An oversight mechanism that enjoys the confidence of parties and electorate is especially pressing in situations of transition, for example, from single- to multi-party systems, or wherever the impartiality of the administrative authorities is in doubt. The effective *institutionalization* of basic electoral and political rights obliges States not only to establish an appropriate electoral system and to implement international obligations in regard to the individual rights, but also,

□ to provide for the holding of legislative elections at regular intervals
□ to establish a neutral, impartial and/or balanced mechanism for the management of legislative elections
□ to establish an effective impartial and non-discriminatory procedure for the registration of voters
□ to lay down by law clear criteria for the registration of voters, such as age, citizenship and residence, and ensure that such criteria are applied without discrimination
□ to lay down by law the regulations governing the formation, registration and functioning of political parties
□ where appropriate in the circumstances, to provide for or regulate the funding of political parties and electoral campaigns, with a view eventually to promoting equality of opportunity
□ to ensure the separation of party and State
□ to establish the conditions for competition in legislative elections on an equitable basis

□ to ensure that electors have a free choice by maintaining the viability of political parties, for example, by public funding and/or guaranteed free time in the media

□ to allow parties and candidates equality of access to government-controlled media

□ to ensure, through national programmes of civic education, that the population become familiar both with election procedures and issues

In addition to implementing measures, States should also take the necessary policy and institutional steps to ensure the achievement of democratic goals and the progressive strengthening of democratic traditions, for example, by establishing a neutral, impartial or balanced mechanism for the management of elections. Any such agency thereby created should,

□ ensure that those responsible for the administration of the election are trained and act impartially

□ ensure that coherent voting procedures are established and made known to the voting public

□ ensure the registration of voters, updating of electoral rolls and balloting procedures, with the assistance of national and international observers, as appropriate

□ encourage parties, candidates and the media to accept and adopt a Code of Conduct to govern the election campaign and the polling period

□ ensure the integrity of the ballot through appropriate measures to prevent double and multiple voting and fraud

□ ensure the integrity of the process for counting votes

□ announce the election results and facilitate any transfer of authority

The principle of the secret ballot implies certain minimum conditions, ranging from the supply of booths and other voting materials, to the location of polling stations and the orderly organization of vote casting. Experience confirms that elections are more likely to be free (that is, the internationally required objective is more likely to be reached), if all major parties have monitors or poll watchers. The State should therefore ensure that,

- voters are able to cast their ballots freely, without fear or intimidation; the authorities should take such steps as are necessary to protect voters from threats or other violence
- the secrecy of the ballot is maintained
- the ballot is conducted so as to avoid fraud or other illegality, and so as to ensure its own security
- the integrity of the process is maintained, and that ballot counting is undertaken by trained personnel, subject to monitoring and/or impartial verification

Under international law, States are obliged to respect and to ensure the human rights of all individuals within their territory and subject to their jurisdiction. This general obligation is particularly important at election times, when the exercise of certain rights is directly related to the goal of a free and fair election at which the will of the people can be expressed. Through its laws and policies, the State and its organs should therefore ensure,

- that freedom of movement, assembly, association and expression are respected, with particular reference to the holding of political rallies and meetings
- that parties and candidates are free to communicate their views to the electorate, and that they enjoy equality of access to State and public service media, which should also provide non-partisan coverage of election campaigns
- that parties and candidates, so far as practicable, enjoy reasonable opportunities to present their electoral platform
- that parties, candidates and supporters enjoy equal security, and that the authorities take the necessary steps to prevent electoral violence

Governments, even unelected ones, also have responsibilities to the communities of which they are a part. In the interests of peaceful change and to protect the rights and freedoms of citizens, governments may therefore have the right and the obligation to limit the rights and activities of those whose conduct constitutes an incitement to violence or otherwise undermines the democratic process. In accordance with the general provisions of international law, however,

□ election rights should only be subject to such restrictions of an exceptional nature which are in accordance with law and reasonably necessary in a democratic society in the interests of national security or public order (*ordre public*), the protection of public health or morals or the protection of the rights and freedoms of others and provided they are consistent with States' obligations under international law.

□ permissible restrictions on candidature, the creation and activity of political parties and campaign rights should not be applied so as to violate the principle of non-discrimination on grounds of race, colour, sex, language, religion, political or other opinion, national or social origin, property, birth or other status.

Finally, a free and fair electoral system must also be able to deal effectively with the different types of complaint that will inevitably arise. The principle of effectiveness of obligations and the human right to a remedy for violations require,

□ that complaints and challenges in electoral matters be determined by an independent and impartial authority, such as an electoral commission or the courts, that decisions be reached promptly, within the timeframe of the election, and that procedures be open and known to the electorate and the parties.

5.   CONCLUSION

At the beginning of this Study, the relatively cautious views of several publicists were cited, particularly in regard to the notion that international law might, or more likely might not, require either representative or democratic government. The present review of State practice and the increasingly *normative* activities of inter-governmental and non-governmental organizations require that this natural caution be reconsidered. This is a time of change, and a time, not necessarily for rejecting, but for re-evaluating traditional doctrine on certain fundamental issues in the system of international organization, including that of entitlement to represent the State.

This may not be the moment to make representative democracy a condition of membership in the society of nations, but it is certainly not too early to assert that the manner by which the will of the people is translated into representative authority has indeed become a proper subject of international law.

Select Bibliography

Alston, P., 'Conjuring up New Human Rights: A Proposal for Quality Control,' 78 *AJIL* 607 (1984).

Atwood, Susan J., Villaveces, Marta Maria. *IFES Technical Election Assistance Project, Romania, March 10-September 29. 1992. Report.* International Foundation for Election Systems. Washington, D.C. 1992.

Brick, A., Gastil, R. & Kimberling, W., *Mongolia: An Assessment of the Election to the Great People's Hural. June 1992.* International Foundation for Election Systems. Washington, D.C. 1992.

Brownlie, I., 'The Rights of Peoples in Modern International Law,' in Crawford, J., ed., *The Rights of Peoples.* Oxford. 1988. 1.

Brunet, G., Marchand, M., et Neher, L., *Togo: Rapport d'évaluation pré-électorale.* International Foundation for Election Systems. 31 mars 1992.

Bulletin de l'Assemblée Nationale, (Paris), no. 7 du 8 juin 1993, 44.

Bulletin de l'Assemblée Nationale, (Paris), no. 8 du 15 juin 1993, 43.

Bulletin de l'Assemblée Nationale, (Paris), no. 14 du 5 oct. 1993, 61.

Bulletin de l'Assemblée Nationale, (Paris), no. 16 du 20 oct. 1993, 44.

Carnahan, R. and Corley, J., 'Czechoslovakia,' in Garber & Bjornlund, *New Democratic Frontier,* 112-34.

Carothers, T., 'Romania,' in Garber & Bjornlund, *New Democratic Frontier,* 75-94.

Cassese, A. and Jouve, E., eds., *Pour un droit des peuples: Essais sur la Déclaration d'Alger.* 1978.

Cassese, A., 'The Self-Determination of Peoples,' in Henkin, L., ed., *The International Bill of Rights-The International Covenant on Civil and Political Rights.* 1981. 92.

Cassese, A., 'Political Self-Determination—Old Concepts and New Developments,' in Cassese, A., ed., *UN Law/Fundamental Rights,* (1979), 137.

Commonwealth Secretariat, *Presidential and National Assembly Elections in Zambia, 31 October 1991.* Report of the Commonwealth Observer Group. 1992.

Commonwealth Secretariat, *The General and Regional Elections in Guyana, 5 October 1992*. Report of the Commonwealth Observer Group. 1992.

Commonwealth Secretariat, *The Presidential Election in Ghana, 3 November 1992*. Report of the Commonwealth Observer Group. 1992.

Commonwealth Secretariat, *Referendum on the Draft Constitution in Seychelles, 12-15 November 1992*. Report of the Commonwealth Observer Group. 1992.

Commonwealth Secretariat, *Parliamentary Elections in Bangladesh, 27 February 1991*. Report of the Commonwealth Observer Group. 1991.

Commonwealth Secretariat, *The Presidential, Parliamentary and Civil Elections in Kenya, 29 December 1992*. Report of the Commonwealth Observer Group. 1993.

Commonwealth Secretariat, *Presidential and National Assembly Elections in Zambia, 31 October 1991*. Report of the Commonwealth Observer Group. 1992.

Commonwealth Secretariat, *General Elections in Malaysia, 20-21 October 1990*. Report of the Commonwealth Observer Group, n.d.

Comprehensive Settlement Agreement for Cambodia, Elections Annex (Annex 3): 31 *Int. Leg. Mat.* 180 (1992).

Cornillon, P. 'Rights and Responsibilities of Election Observers,' Inter-Parliamentary Union. Geneva. Paper presented to the International Conference of La Laguna on Freedom of Elections and the International Observation of Elections, Tenerife, 27 Feb.-2 Mar. 1994.

Council of Europe, Report of Delegation to Lithuania in October and November 1992: CE Doc. 6724, Add. II. 20 Jan. 1993.

Council of Europe, *Handbook for Observers of Elections*, Strasbourg. 1992.

Council of Freely Elected Heads of Government. *Observing Guyana's Electoral Process 1990-1992*. Special Report #3. Carter Center of Emory University. Atlanta. Georgia. 1992.

Council of Freely Elected Heads of Government. Carter Center of Emory University. *Electoral Reform in Mexico*. Occasional Paper Series. Vol. IV, No. 1. Carter Center of Emory University. Atlanta. Georgia. Nov. 1993.

Council of Freely Elected Heads of Government. National Democratic Institute for International Affairs. *1990 Elections in the Dominican Republic: Report of an Observer Delegation*. Special Report #2. National Democratic Institute. Carter Center of Emory University. Atlanta. Georgia. 1990.

Council of Freely Elected Heads of Government. *Observing Nicaragua's Elections, 1989-1990.* Special Report #1. Carter Center of Emory University. Atlanta. Georgia. 1990.

Courtney, John C., 'Introduction,' in Courtney, John C., ed., *Registering Voters: Comparative Perspectives,* The Center for International Affairs. Harvard University, (1991), 1.

Crawford, J., 'The Rights of Peoples: "Peoples" or "Governments"?' in Crawford, J., ed., *The Rights of Peoples.* Oxford. (1988). 55.

CSCE, Declaration on Principles Guiding Relations between Participating States, Helsinki Final Act, 1 Aug. 1975: text in 1975 *Digest of United States Practice in International Law*, 8.

CSCE, Document of the Copenhagen Meeting of the Conference on the Human Dimension: 29 June 1990: 29 *Int. Leg. Mat.* 1305 (1990).

CSCE, Office for Democratic Institutions and Human Rights, 'International Observation of the Referendum held in the Russian Federation on April 25, 1993'. 1993.

Department of State, *Country Reports on Human Rights Practices for 1988,* Report submitted to the Senate Committee on Foreign Relations and the House Committee on Foreign Affairs, 101st Cong., 1st Sess., 155-68 (1989).

Edsall, Thomas B. and Gladwell, Malcolm, 'Probe Begins on NJ "Vote Suppressing" Claim,' *The Guardian Weekly*, 21 Nov. 1993.

European Centre for Parliamentary Research and Documentation, *Electoral System Legislation. National Reports: Parts One and Two*. May 1993.

Fawcett, J.E.S., *The Application of the European Convention on Human Rights.* Oxford. 2nd ed. 1987.

Fischer, Jeffrey, 'Voter Registration in Emerging Democracies. Two Case Studies: Haiti 1990; Guyana 1991,' in Courtney, John C., ed. *Registering Voters: Comparative Perspectives.* The Center for International Affairs. Harvard University, (1991), 55.

Fox, G.H., 'The Right to Political Participation in International Law,' 17 *Yale J. Int'l Law* 539 (1992).

Franck, T.M., 'The Emerging Right to Democratic Governance,' 86 *AJIL* 46 (1992).

Gaja, G., 'L'autodetermination politique dans la Déclaration d'Alger: objectifs et réalités,' in Cassese, A. & Jouve, E., eds., *Pour un droit des peuples*. 1978.

Garber, L., 'The OAU and Elections,' 4 *Journal of Democracy* 55 (1993).

Garber, L., 'The Role of International Observers,' in Garber & Bjornlund, *New Democratic Frontier*, 211.

Garber, L., 'Bulgaria,' in Garber & Bjornlund, *New Democratic Frontier*, 135-60.

Garber, L. and Bjornlund, E., eds., *The New Democratic Frontier. A Country by Country Report on Elections in Central and Eastern Europe*. National Democratic Institute for International Affairs, Washington, D.C. 1992.

Garber, L. and Cowan, G., 'The Virtues of Parallel Vote Tabulations,' 4 *Journal of Democracy* 95 (1993).

Garber L. and Gibson, C., *Review of United Nations Electoral Assistance 1992-93*. New York. Aug. 1993.

Goodwin-Gill, G.S., 'Obligations of Conduct and Result,' in P. Alston and K. Tomaševski, eds., *The Right to Food*, 1985, 111-8.

Gordon, D. & Reinke, F., 'East Germany,' in Garber & Bjornlund, *New Democratic Frontier,* 20-38.

Grisel, E., *Initiative et Référendum Populaires: Traité de la démocratie semi-directe en droit Suisse*. Dorigny. 1987.

Gros Espiell, H., 'Liberté des Elections et Observation Internationale des Elections,' mimeo., Conférence international de la Laguna, Tenerife, 27 févr.-2 mars 1994.

Human Rights Watch and Lawyers Committee for Human Rights, *Critique: Review of the Department of State's Country Reports on Human Rights Practices for 1988*. 1989.

Inter-Parliamentary Union, *Chronicle of Parliamentary Elections and Developments*, No. 24, 1989-1990.

Inter-Parliamentary Union, *Chronicle of Parliamentary Elections and Developments*, No. 25, 1990-1991.

Inter-Parliamentary Union, *Chronicle of Parliamentary Elections and Developments*, No. 26, 1991-1992.

Inter-Parliamentary Union, *Chronicle of Parliamentary Elections and Developments*, No. 27, 1992-1993.

Inter-Parliamentary Union, *Electoral Systems: A World-Wide Comparative Survey*. Geneva. 1993.

Inter-Parliamentary Union, Questionnaire concerning Parliamentary Elections: IPU doc. CHR/93/1.

Inter-Parliamentary Union, *Report of IPU Election Observer Mission, Cambodia, 16 May-4 June 1993*. Geneva. 1993.

Inter-Parliamentary Union, *Report of the Mission to Observe the Elections in Namibia*: IPU doc. CL/146/10-R.1. 20 Dec. 1989.

International Republican Institute, *Kenya: The December 29, 1992 Elections*. 1993.

Kimberling, William C., 'A Rational Approach to Evaluating Alternative Voter Registration Systems and Procedures,', in Courtney, John C., ed. *Registering Voters: Comparative Perspectives*. The Center for International Affairs. Harvard University, (1991), 3.

Laundy, P. *Parliaments in the Modern World*. Dartmouth. Aldershot. 1989.

Masclet, Jean-Claude, *Droit électoral*. Presses Universitaires de France. Paris. 1989.

McGoldrick, D., *The Human Rights Committee*. Oxford. 1991.

Melia, T.O., 'Hungary,' in Garber & Bjornlund, *New Democratic Frontier*, 39-64.

Merloe, P., *Election Campaign Broadcasting in Transitional Democracies: Problems, Principles and Guidelines*. Prepared for Articel 19, the International Centre against Censorship. Pre-publication draft. August 1993.

Merrills, J.G., *The Development of International Law by the European Court of Human Rights*. Manchester. 1988.

Nadais, A., 'Choice of Electoral Systems,' in Garber, Larry and Bjornlund, Eric, eds., *The New Democratic Frontier. A country by country report on elections in Central and Eastern Europe*. National Democratic Institute for International Affairs, Washington, D.C. 1992. 190-203.

National Democratic Institute for International Affairs. National Republican Institute for International Affairs. *The June 1990 Elections in Bulgaria*. International Delegation Report. Washington, D.C. 1990.

National Democratic Institute for International Affairs. *The October 1990 Elections in Pakistan*. Report of the International Delegation. Washington, D.C. 1991.

National Democratic Institute for International Affairs. Carter Center of Emory University. *The October 31 1991 National Elections in Zambia*. Washington, D.C. 1992.

National Democratic Institute for International Affairs. 'Preliminary Statement. NDI International Observer Delegation to the Pakistan National Elections'. 8 Oct. 1993.

National Democratic Institute for International Affairs. Council of Freely Elected Heads of Government. 'Preliminary Post-Election Statement. International Delegation to the National Elections in Paraguay.' Asunción. 10 May 1993.

National Democratic Institute for International Affairs. *An Assessment of the Senegalese Electoral Code*. International Delegation Report. Washington, D.C. 1991.

National Democratic Institute for International Affairs. 'Executive Summary. February 21, 1993 Presidential Elections in Senegal.' International Delegation Report. Washington, D.C. 1993.

National Democratic Institute for International Affairs. *An Assessment of the October 11, 1992 Election in Cameroon*. Washington, D.C. 1993.

National Election Monitoring Unit (NEMU), *The Multi-Party General Elections in Kenya*. 1993.

Norwegian Helsinki Committee. Norwegian Institute of Human Rights. *Manual for Election Observation*. Mimeo. Draft. Oslo. 1993.

Organization of American States Secretary-General, *Observation of the Electoral Process, Nicaragua 1989-90, Observers' Guide*. Washington, D.C. 1989.

Pinto-Duschinsky, M., 'The Role of Political Parties,' in International Foundation for Election Systems. *Central European Electoral Systems Symposium, Budapest, July 30-August 2, 1991*. International Foundation for Election Systems. Washington, D.C., (1991), 74.

Schweizer, R.J., 'Zur Stellung der Schweiz gegenüber Art. 3 der Zusatzprotokolls zur Europäischer Menschenrechtskonvention (Gewährleistung von freien und geheimen Wahlen), 41.

Shelton, D., 'Representative Democracy and Human Rights in the Western Hemisphere,' 12 *Human Rights Law Journal* 353 (1991).

Sieghart, P., *The International Law of Human Rights*. Oxford. 1983.

Steiner, H.J., 'Political Participation as a Human Right,' 1 *Harv. H.R.YB* 77 (1988).

UN/UNDP: *Guidelines on Special Arrangements for Electoral Assistance*. New York. Aug. 1992.

United Nations, *Vienna Declaration and Programme of Action*: UN doc. A/CONF.157/23, 12 Jul. 1993.

United Nations, *Guidelines for Member States Considering the Formulation of a Request for Electoral Assistance*, New York. n.d.

United Nations, *Report of the Joint International Observer Group on the Malawi National Referendum*, New York. 14 Jun. 1993.

United Nations, Report of the Secretary-General, *Enhancing the effectiveness of the principle of periodic and genuine elections*: UN doc. A/47/668, 18 Nov. 1992.

United Nations, Report of the Secretary-General, *Enhancing the effectiveness of the principle of periodic and genuine elections:* UN doc. A/46/609, 19 Nov. 1991.

United Nations, *Establishment and Terms of Reference of the United Nations Observer Mission to Verify the Electoral Process in Nicaragua (ONUVEN)*: UN doc. A/44/375 (1989).

US Commission on Security and Cooperation in Europe. *Russia's Parliamentary Election and Constitutional Referendum, December 12, 1993*. Washington, D.C. Jan. 1994.

US Commission on Security and Cooperation in Europe. *Elections in Central and Eastern Europe*. A Compendium of Reports on the Elections Held from March through June 1990. Washington, D.C. Jul. 1990.

US Commission on Security and Cooperation in Europe. *Elections in the Baltic States and Soviet Republics*. A Compendium of Reports on Parliamentary Elections Held in 1990. Washington, D.C. Dec. 1990.

Vasak, K., 'Freedom of Elections and the International Observation of Elections,' mimeo., Instituto Tricontental de la Democracia Parlamentaria y de los Derechos Humanos de la Universidad de la Laguna, n.d.

Vasak, K., 'Les normes internationales existantes relatives aux elections et leur mise en oeuvre,' mimeo., n.d.

Villiger, M.E., *Handbuch der Europäischer Menschenrechtskonvention (EMRK)*. Zurich. 1993.

Wolfinger, Raymond E., 'The Politics of Voter Registration Reform,' in Courtney, John C., ed., *Registering Voters: Comparative Perspectives,* The Center for International Affairs. Harvard University, (1991), 28.

ANNEX 1:

FREE AND FAIR ELECTIONS —EXTRACTS FROM SELECTED INTERNATIONAL INSTRUMENTS

1948 Universal Declaration of Human Rights

Article 21

(1) Everyone has the right to take part in the government of his country, directly or through freely chosen representatives.

(2) Everyone has the right of equal access to public service in his country.

(3) The will of the people shall be the basis of the authority of government; this will shall be expressed in periodic and genuine elections which shall be by universal and equal suffrage and shall be held by secret vote or by equivalent free voting procedures.

1952 Convention on the Political Rights of Women

Article 1

Women shall be entitled to vote in all elections on equal terms with men, without any discrimination.

1965 Convention on the Elimination of All Forms of Racial Discrimination

Article 5

In compliance with the fundamental obligations laid down in article 2 of this Convention, States Parties undertake to prohibit and to eliminate racial discrimination in all its forms and to guarantee the right of everyone, without distinction as to race, colour, or national or ethnic origin, to equality before the law, notably in the enjoyment of the following rights:
...

(c) Political rights, in particular the rights to participate in elections - to vote and to stand for election - on the basis of universal and equal suffrage, to take part in the Government as well as in the conduct of public affairs at any level and to have equal access to public service;

(d) Other civil rights, in particular:

(viii) The right to freedom of opinion and expression;

(ix) The right to freedom of peaceful assembly and association;

1966 Covenant on Civil and Political Rights

Article 25

Every citizen shall have the right and the opportunity, without any of the distinctions mentioned in article 2 and without unreasonable restrictions:

(a) To take part in the conduct of public affairs, directly or through freely chosen representatives;

(b) To vote and to be elected at genuine periodic elections which shall be by universal and equal suffrage and shall be held by secret ballot, guaranteeing the free expression of the will of the electors;

(c) To have access, on general terms of equality, to public service in his country.

1979 Convention on the Elimination of All Forms of Discrimination against Women

Article 7

State Parties shall take all appropriate measures to eliminate discrimination against women in the political and public life of the country and, in particular, shall ensure to women, on equal terms with men, the right:

(a) To vote in all elections and public referenda and to be eligible for selection to all publicly elected bodies;

(b) To participate in the formulation of government policy and the implementation thereof and to hold public office and perform all public functions at all levels of government;

(c) To participate in non-governmental organizations and associations concerned with the public and political life of the country.

1948 American Declaration of the Rights and Duties of Man

Article 20

Every person having legal capacity is entitled to participate in the government of his country, directly or through his representatives, and to take part in popular elections, which shall be by secret ballot, and shall be honest, periodic and free.

1950 European Convention on Human Rights: Protocol 1

Article 3

The High Contracting Parties undertake to hold free elections at reasonable intervals by secret ballot, under conditions which will ensure the free expression of the opinion of the people in the choice of the legislature.

1969 American Convention on Human Rights

Article 23: Right to Participate in Government

1. Every citizen shall enjoy the following rights and opportunities:

(a) to take part in the conduct of public affairs, directly or through freely chosen representatives;

(b) to vote and to be elected in genuine periodic elections, which shall be by universal and equal suffrage and by secret ballot that guarantees the free expression of the will of the voters; and

(c) to have access, under general conditions of equality, to the public service of his country.

2. The law may regulate the exercise of the rights and opportunities referred to in the preceding paragraph only on the basis of age, nationality, residence, language, education, civil and mental capacity, or sentencing by a competent court in criminal proceedings.

1981 African Charter on Human and Peoples' Rights

Article 13

1. Every citizen shall have the right to participate freely in the government of his country, either directly or through freely chosen representatives in accordance with the provisions of the law.

2. Every citizen shall have the right of equal access to the public service of his country.

3. Every individual shall have the right of access to public property and services in strict equality of all persons before the law.

ANNEX 2:

ELECTION CODES OF CONDUCT-SELECTED EXAMPLES
CAMBODIA[1]

CODE OF CONDUCT

1.   All persons, all political parties, their leaders, members and supporters, all provisionally and officially registered political parties, their leaders, members, supporters and candidates, shall abide by this Code of Conduct.

2.   All political parties are entitled to and shall enjoy, the fundamental right of a free and fair election, including the freedom to campaign.

3.   All political parties shall respect the right and freedom of all other parties to campaign, and disseminate their political ideas and principles without fear.

4.   In particular, all political parties, officially and provisionally registered political parties, their leaders, members, supporters and candidates shall obey the following rules:

(1) Intimidation, in whatever form, shall be prohibited, and manuals, instructions and orders of political parties and provisionally and officially registered political parties shall reinforce and emphasize this prohibition.

(2) The possession and use of any weapon of any kind, or of any instrument capable of use as a weapon, at any political rally, meeting, march or demonstration shall be prohibited. Parties' manuals, instructions and orders shall reinforce this prohibition.

(3) Parties and candidates shall inform the local UNTAC office of any planned public meetings or political rallies, and shall in good faith take all necessary steps to avoid violent confrontation or conflict between their supporters, and shall comply with all directions, instructions or orders issued by UNTAC in relation to such meetings.

(4) All parties shall avoid the coincidence, in time or place, of their meetings, rallies, marches or demonstrations with those of other parties, and to this end shall liaise and cooperate with UNTAC and with other parties.

(5) All parties, their members and supporters, shall refrain from disrupting the meetings, marches or demonstrations of other parties.

1   Inter-Parliamentary Union, 'Report of the IPU Election Observer Mission, Camdodia, 16 May-4 June 1993,' Geneva, (1993), Annex II.

(6) Parties and candidates shall at all times avoid, in speeches, broadcasts, pamphlets, newsletters, press statements, posters, their party platforms, campaign advertisements or otherwise, using inflammatory language or other language which threatens or incites violence in any form against others.

(7) All political parties shall refrain from obstructing persons from attending the meetings, marches or rallies of other parties.

(8) All parties shall refrain from plagiarising the symbols of other parties, and shall not steal, destroy or disfigure the political or other campaign material or posters of other parties, or the election information material of UNTAC.

(9) All political parties, and especially their leaders, shall ensure freedom of access of other parties to all potential voters on public or private property, in camps or reception centres, or wherever they may be. Parties shall ensure that potential voters wishing to participate in political activities are free to do so.

(10) All parties shall consistently reinforce and emphasize to their supporters and to all voters that the ballot will be secret, and that no person will know how any individual has voted.

(11) All parties shall establish effective communication with one another at the central, provincial and district levels, and shall appoint liaison personnel, to be available for this purpose at all times, to deal with any problem arising during registration of voters, the campaign or the polling.

(12) All parties shall attend at least once every two weeks a meeting under the chairmanship of the Chief Electoral Officer to discuss any matters of concern relating to the campaign. In addition, a standing committee of leaders of registered political parties shall attend at least every two weeks a meeting under the chairmanship of the Special Representative or his deputy to deal with matters of concern relating to the campaign. The above-mentioned meetings shall commence from a date to be determined by the Special Representative.

(13) All parties shall bring all information or complaints regarding intimidation or other allegations of unlawful conduct immediately to the attention of UNTAC.

(14) Parties shall not abuse the right to complain, nor make false, frivolous or vexatious complaints.

(15) All parties shall cooperate fully with the Special Representatives's Electoral Advisory Committee.

(16) All parties shall issue instructions and orders to their members and supporters to observe the Electoral Law, this Code, the instructions of UNTAC officials, and all orders and directives of the Special Representative, and take all necessary steps in good faith to ensure compliance with the Electoral law and this Code.

(17) The Special Representative and all parties shall publicize this Code and the electoral law throughout Cambodia by all means at their disposal.

SEYCHELLES[2]

Code of Conduct to be Adhered to by Political Parties, their Members and Supporters on an Election or Referendum

This Code of Conduct is aimed at maintaining a peaceful atmosphere during an election or referendum campaign and on polling day.

CODE OF CONDUCT

1. Existing election laws and rules must be adhered to.

2. All political parties and contestants will have to extend all necessary help and co-operation to the law-enforcing authorities.

3. Everyone should be aware not only of his own rights, but should also respect the rights of others.

4. All political parties and candidates participating in the polls will extend full co-operation to election officials and ensure their safety until the polls are over.

5. Election campaigns should be so organised that a congenial and peaceful atmosphere prevails during polling.

6. It is expected that criticism of opponents will occur during electioneering. All parties shall exercise restraint in speech, manner and conduct, and show respect for the opinion of others so that electioneering does not turn into a war of words and confrontation.

7. It is expected that criticism of opponents will occur during electioneering. However, indecorous and provocative speeches, statements, posters, taunting, ridiculing and innuendoes shall be avoided. Parties shall be careful so that behaviour, statements or comments do not cause unnecessary tension.

8. All political parties shall be vocal against violence. No party shall give indulgence to any kind of violent activity to demonstrate party strength or to prove supremacy. All political parties will extend co-operation to the law-enforcing agencies for recovery of illegal arms. No party will take any initiative for the release of any person arrested by police with arms during an election or referendum campaign or in the polling station during voting or in the vicinity of the polling station during polls.

2   Commonwealth Secretariat, *Referendum on the Draft Constitution in Seychelles, 12-15 November 1992*. Report of the Commonwealth Observer Group, (1992), Annex VII

9. All parties and candidates will have equal opportunity for publicity. Meetings, processions and other campaign activities of opponents cannot be interfered with. Posters and banners shall be displayed only in accordance with the Code of Conduct set out in the Schedule hereto.

10. Assistance of the nearest law-enforcing agencies will have to be sought to resist and check any sort of election offence.

11. Any attempts to influence voting through money or allurement are election offences. Everyone should be aware of these offences.

12. No Government transport shall be used to carry voters to polling stations other than persons working for Government departments who are on duty or persons living in Government institutions. This rule does not apply to a person who has the use of a Government vehicle and the vehicle is used for self and family.

13. No Defence Force vehicles shall be used to carry voters, including Defence Force personnel, to polling stations.

14. Defence Force personnel shall not go to vote in their uniform.

15. Political parties will not procure votes by forcible occupation of polling stations or through illegal activities in the polling stations.

16. No candidate or party can commit or give covertly or overtly any contribution, grant or favour to any individual, institution, body or organization until election or referendum day for the purpose of election campaigning and obtaining votes.

17. The congenial and peaceful atmosphere for an election or a referendum cannot be disturbed by spreading untrue and motivated rumour or by having recourse to conspiracy.

18. No election camps, check points and refreshment stalls shall be set up by political parties, their members and supporters. There shall be no campaigning of any sort either individually or collectively on polling day. District Council offices shall be closed on the day of the election or referendum. Voters must be left alone when queuing up so that they are not influenced in any way.

19. Where a voter is incapacitated by blindness or other physical cause or otherwise, he may ask the Electoral Officer to record his vote in the presence of a person selected by him. In those circumstances the Electoral Officer shall satisfy himself that: (a) the voter is truly incapacitated as he claims to be; (b) that the person who is to witness the vote has been freely and genuinely chosen by the voter; and (c) that the vote expressed by the voter is free. In this respect the political parties shall not abuse this procedure to pressure incapacitated persons to vote in their favour.

20. In addition to election officials, only the voters are entitled to enter the 'polling stations.' The political parties shall make sure that their workers do not enter the polling stations and loiter therein. Only the polling and counting agents will remain seated at their designated seats in the polling station and discharge their responsibility from there. No disruption shall be caused by the moving or changing of accredited agents.

CODE OF CONDUCT RELATING TO POSTERS AND BANNERS

1.0 Use of Bulletin Boards

1.1 Any elections or referendum notice, political advertisement or announcement shall be displayed only on bulletin boards.

1.2 These bulletin boards or hoardings will be erected only at certain specific places agreed upon by the Land Transport Division, Police (Traffic Section) and Planning Authority.

1.3 The Planning Authority, Police (Traffic Section) and Land Transport Division shall agree on the size, height and number of the boards to be displayed in a particular area.

1.4 The Department of Tourism and Transport (Tourism Division) has already erected some permanent bill boards in Victoria. Only advertisements announcing local events such as educational, cultural, social or recreational and tourism-promoting activities should be displayed on these boards.

1.5 Extra bulletin boards (temporary) may be erected and allocated to the different political parties.

1.6 Boards will be erected only 14 days prior to the day of the election or referendum.

1.7 All boards and political displays must be removed by the political parties as soon as possible, in any case within 14 days of the close of the poll in the election or referendum in accordance with regulation 13 (2) (b) of the Town and Country Planning (Control of Advertisements) Regulations, Cap 160.

2.0 Use of Cloth Banners

2.1 Easily removable cloth banners should be utilised as much as possible instead of pasted paper posters.

2.2 Cloth banners shall be displayed only after the necessary permission has been obtained from the Land Transport Division and Police (Traffic Section).

2.3 All banners shall be removed as soon as possible, in any case, within 14 days after the election or referendum.

3.0 Use of Paint

3.1 There shall be a total ban on the use of paint (liquids and sprays) to write upon, mark or paint any slogan on any road, pavement, telephone or electric posts, wall, or fence, etc., whether on public or private property.

This is an offence punishable under Section 183 (j) of the Penal Code, Cap 73.

4.0 Electoral or Referendum Posters

4.1 Electoral or Referendum posters shall be affixed only on special boards erected for this purpose as set out in paragraph 1.

4.2 No poster or any other paper shall be pasted on any wall, building, road, pavement, telephone or electric poles, or fence whether public or private property.

This is an offence punishable under Section 183 (j) of the Penal Code, Cap 73.

5.0 Respect of Others and their Property

5.1 Political party members and supporters shall respect others and their property and shall refrain from causing damage to any property whether public or private.

GHANA[3]

CODE OF CONDUCT

Code of Conduct for Political Parties in Ghana for Public Elections

The Registered Political Parties of Ghana realising the need for a Code of Conduct for their activities during public elections hereby make this Code of Conduct which shall be adhered to by all political parties:

1. Existing election laws and rules must be complied with by all political parties.

2. All political parties and contestants shall extend all necessary help and co-operation to the law-enforcing authorities.

3. Everyone should not only be aware of his rights, but should also respect the rights of others.

4. All political parties and candidates participating in the polls shall extend full co-operation to the election officials and ensure their safety and security before, during and after the polls.

5. Election campaigns should be so organised that a congenial and peaceful atmosphere prevails during polling.

6. The political parties shall not propagate any opinion, or action which in any manner is prejudicial to the sovereignty, integrity or security of Ghana, or the maintenance of public order, or the integrity or independence of the judiciary of Ghana or which defies or brings into ridicule the judiciary or the armed forces of Ghana, or which is immoral.

7. The political parties, their candidates, agents or workers shall not obstruct or break up meetings organised by rival parties and candidates, nor interrupt speeches or prevent distribution of handbills, leaflets and pasting of posters of other parties and candidates and shall not destroy or deface posters of other parties.

8. Political parties shall avoid criticism of other political parties, their leaders and candidates on matters that have no bearing an their public activities. Criticism and comments shall be confined to policies and programmes of the parties. Speeches and slogans shall be dignified and based on principles of morality, decorum and decency.

9. Political parties shall refrain from speeches calculated to arouse parochial feelings and controversy or conflicts between sects, communities and ethnic groups.

3   Commonwealth Secretariat, *The Presidential Election in Ghana, 3 November 1992*. Report of the Commonwealth Observer Group, (1992), Annex XVII.

10.   Public leaders and all other participants in political activity shall act with a sense or responsibility and dignity benefitting their status. While propagating their own views and programmes, they shall not interfere with the freedom of others to do the same as that would be the negation of democracy.

11.   Appeals to violence or resort to violence during meetings, processions, or during polling hours shall be strictly avoided.

12.   Carriage of dangerous and lethal weapons shall not be allowed in public meetings and official regulations in this regard shall be strictly observed. Use of fire crackers and other explosives at public meetings shall not be allowed.

13.   Political parties and their candidates shall extend co-operation to the officers on election duty in order to ensure peaceful and orderly polling and complete freedom for the voters to exercise their franchise without being subject to any annoyance or obstruction.

14.   Political parties and their candidates shall scrupulously avoid all activities which amount to 'corrupt practices' and offences under the electoral laws; such as bribing of voters, intimidation of voters, impersonation of voters, canvassing within 500 metres of a polling station.

15.   Political parties, their candidates, agents or workers shall not indulge in offering gifts or gratification or inducing another to stand or not to stand as a candidate, or to withdraw or not to withdraw his candidature.

16.   Political parties and their candidates shall not procure the support or assistance of any public servant or official of the Electoral Commission to promote or hinder the election of a candidate.

17.   Political parties and their candidates should not procure the support of sympathizers to destroy ballot paper or any official mark on the ballot paper.

18.   Notwithstanding any of the above, all political parties shall be vocal against violence. No party shall give indulgence to any kind of violent activity to demonstrate parry strength or to prove supremacy. All political parties will extend co-operation to the law enforcing agencies for recovery of illegal arms. No party shall take any initiative for the release of any person arrested by police with arms during election campaign or in the polling centre during voting or in the vicinity of the polling centre during polls.

19.   Assistance of the nearest law-enforcing agencies, namely, the police, Ghana Armed Forces, the Fire Service and the Prison Services shall be sought to resist and check any election offence.

20.   Political parties will reach an understanding to resist attempts to procure votes by forcible occupation of polling centres or illegal activities in the polling centres, by any person. Votes thus obtained illegally will be of no use as the Electoral Commission will cancel polling in such centres.

21.   The congenial and peaceful atmosphere for election must not be disturbed by spreading untrue and motivated rumour or by taking recourse to conspiracy.

22.   On the declaration of a free and fair election by the Commission to the satisfaction of the majority of the political parties, invited persons and recognised observers, losing candidates will honourably concede defeat.

For this Code of Conduct to enjoy maximum respect by the agents and supporters of the political parties, it must be seen to be endorsed by all the presidential candidates and all the chairpersons of the political parties.

To this end, this Code shall be launched by the Electoral Commission together with all the Presidential Candidates contesting the 1992 elections and the Chairpersons of the political parties.

Made at Accra 23rd day of October, 1992.

GUYANA[4]

GUIDELINES FOR MEDIA AND POLITICAL PARTIES

1. Contextual Background

Freedom of expression by the media — radio, television and print — is a symbol of democracy. The manner in which the media use their freedom carries an obligation to serve the society and public as a whole. Because of this need to serve the public, the media inherit a public trust. The media have a responsibility to conduct their operations at all times in a professional manner and to exercise critical and discerning judgment which respects and advances the rights and dignity of all people and maintains standards of good taste as reflected by the society and public served. The media must enrich the daily life of the people they serve through information, education and entertainment; they must provide for the fair discussion of matters of public concern; engage in works directed toward the common good; and volunteer aid and comfort in times of stress and emergency.

2. General Guidelines during the Campaign Period[5]

(a) News
News reporting should be factual, fair and without bias. Professional care should be maintained in the use and selection of news sources. News analysis, commentary and editorials should be clearly identified as such, distinguishing them from straight news reporting.

(b) Controversial Public Issues
Expressions of responsible views on public issues of a controversial nature should give fair representation to opposing sides of issues. Requests by individuals, groups or organizations to present their views on controversial public issues should be considered on the basis of their individual merits and in the light of their contributions to the public interest.

3. Specific Guidelines for the Campaign Period

(a) Access by Political Parties
During the Campaign Period, the media have a special responsibility to the public to encourage participation by the electorate in the democratic process and to ensure they have the opportunity to be informed on the candidates and issues. To enable this, the Guyana Elections Commission

---

4   Commonwealth Secretariat, *The General and Regional Elections in Guyana, 5 October 1992*. Report of the Commonwealth Observer Group (1992), Annex X.
5   The official campaign period for these Guidelines is defined as that time between Nomination Day and Election Day.

requests that the broadcast media — radio and television — make available at no cost a minimum of five minutes of prime time weekly to each political party with candidates for national office, and also requests that daily publication print media make available at no cost 10 column inches of space weekly to each qualified political party. The Chairman of the Elections Commission shall notify the media of the Parties that qualify for this free coverage. All such programs and columns should be clearly identified as a public service political message prepared by the (name) political party and unedited by the (media). The (name) political party is solely responsible for its content. Programs and messages exceeding the free time and space allocations may be rejected or returned to the Party. The media may establish reasonable deadlines for submission of the materials in order to fit their broadcast or publication schedules. The media shall ensure all Parties are given equal treatment and access as to time and location of these messages. Concerning access to radio broadcasts, in order to provide complete geographic coverage, it may be necessary to repeat the programs at a different time and frequency.

(b) Paid Political Messages
Political parties or candidates who wish additional time and space should pay for all messages or advertisements at current established rates — preferably the lowest published rate — but each Party should be charged the same rate.

Further the media must ensure that all Parties and candidates have equal access to the broadcast times and schedule for broadcast media; and similar equitable access, space and location, for print media. One political Party or candidate should not be allowed to block access by other Parties or candidates by purchasing all availabilities of time or space.

Equitable and fair treatment of all Parties and candidates must be the standard adhered to by all media. While the above addresses equitable treatment concerning broadcast or publication of the messages, the same standard must be applied to any production in preparation for broadcast or publication.

Payment terms for political advertisements should be the same for all Parties utilizing the industry standard of cash in advance. All paid political messages should carry a statement that they are a 'Paid Political Advertisement'.

(c) Correction of Media Errors
Broadcast or publication errors beyond the control of the medium, i.e. mechanical failure or act of God, should be corrected in accordance with the standard broadcast or publication policies of procedures for the

correction of mistakes. The media may not censor, change or alter in any manner any of the materials presented by the Parties or candidates for broadcast or publication by the media.

(d) Questionable Materials

In the event any of the media believe a political message may not be in good taste, or contrary to the public interest, security, peace or morality, the questioned political message may be rejected by the media. However the media must provide specific details to the Party as to the reason for rejection and allow the material to be changed to meet broadcast or publication standards.

(e) Disclaimers

The media shall insert or broadcast a disclaimer daily when any free or paid political messages will be carried published by their medium. For example: 'The political messages or advertisements published in today's newspaper are prepared by the Political Party or candidate without editing or change and do not necessarily reflect the opinion of this newspaper.' One insert anywhere in the newspaper should be sufficient. A similar statement shall be made by the broadcast media at least once during the broadcast day and not necessarily immediately preceding or following broadcast of political material.

BANGLADESH[6]

Jatiya Sangsad (Parliament) Election, 1991

Code of Conduct to be Adhered to by Political Parties

The code of conduct, finalised after discussions with the representatives of 67 political parties including major ones, is aimed at maintaining a peaceful atmosphere during the election campaign and on polling day. The Election Commission hoped that if all political parties faithfully abide by the code, they would greatly contribute to the holding of a credible election in the country. Legitimacy of a representative government elected through such an election will not be questioned.

CODE OF CONDUCT

1. Existing election laws and rules must be adhered to.

2. All political parties and contestants will have to extend all necessary help and co-operation to the law-enforcing authorities.

3. Everyone should be aware of not only his own rights, but should also respect the rights of others.

4. All political parties and candidates participating in the polls will extend full co-operation to the election officials and ensure their safety and security until the polls are over.

5. lection campaigns should be so organised that a congenial and peaceful atmosphere prevails during polling.

6. Nothing should be done that will create tension and disrupt the congenial atmosphere of the election. All parties should exercise restraint in speech and show respect to the opinions of others so that electioneering does not turn into war of words.

7. It is expected that criticism of opponents will occur during electioneering. However, indecorous and provocative speeches/ statements, taunting, ridiculing and innuendos should be avoided. Parties should be careful so that statements or comments do not cause unnecessary tension. In case a situation for the possibility of a clash arises because of a misunderstanding between contesting parties, then an Election Co-ordination Committee composed of representatives from the concerned parties shall allay tension and settle the dispute.

6   Commonwealth Secretariat, *Parliamentary Elections in Bangladesh, 27 February 1991*. Report of the Commonwealth Observer Group, (1991), Annex 7.

8. All political parties shall be vocal against violence. No party shall give indulgence to any kind of violent activity to demonstrate party strength or to prove supremacy. All political parties will extend co-operation to the law enforcing agencies for recovery of illegal arms. No party will take any initiative for the release of any person arrested by police with arms during election campaign or in the polling centre during voting or in the vicinity of the polling centre during polls.

9. All parties and candidates will have equal opportunity for publicity. Meetings, processions and other campaign activities of opponents cannot be interfered with.

10. Assistance of the nearest law enforcing agencies will have to be sought to resist and check any sort of election offence.

11. Any attempts to influence voting through money or allurement and to hire or use any kind of transport to carry voters other than for self and family are election offences. Everyone should be aware of these offences.

12. Political parties will reach an understanding to resist attempts to procure votes by forcible occupation of polling centres or thorough illegal activities in the polling centres. Votes thus obtained illegally will be of no use as the Election Commission will cancel polling in such centres.

13. No candidate can commit covertly or overtly any contribution or grant to any institution in his constituency until election day for the purpose of election campaigning and obtaining votes.

14. The congenial and peaceful atmosphere for election can not be disturbed by spreading untrue and motivated rumour or by taking recourse to conspiracy.

15. Election camps cannot be set up within the prohibited area or close to the polling centres and no campaign shall be allowed inside the polling centres.

16. In addition to the election officials, only the voters are entitled to enter the polling centres: the political parties should make sure that their workers do not enter the polling centres and loiter therein. Only the polling agents will remain seated at their designated seats in the polling centre and discharge their responsibility from there.

Index